MW00851072

GODZILLA

Published in 2022 by Welbeck

An Imprint of Welbeck Non-Fiction Limited, part of Welbeck Publishing Group.
Based in London and Sydney.
www.welbeckpublishing.com

TM & © TOHO CO., LTD.

Text & Design © Welbeck Non-Fiction Limited, part of Welbeck Publishing Group.
Images copyright © 2022 TOHO CO., LTD

All rights reserved. No part of this publication may be reproduced, stored in a retrieval system, or transmitted in any form or by any means, electronically, mechanical, photocopying, recording or otherwise, without the prior permission of the copyright owners and the publishers.

A CIP catalogue record for this book is available from the British Library

ISBN 978 1 78739 899 3

Editors: Roland Hall, Ross Hamilton
Design: Russell Knowles, Emma Wicks
Production: Rachel Burgess

Printed in China

10 9 8 7 6 5

THE OFFICIAL GUIDE TO THE KING OF THE MONSTERS

GRAHAM SKIPPER

CONTENTS

INTRODUCTION

In 1954, the world was introduced to a monster that would terrify millions, level entire cities, and battle dozens of other giant creatures for over 60 years. Godzilla emerged from the sea and quickly became a cinematic icon, going on to star in over 30 feature films, as well as television series, comic books, video games, and more. It would earn a star on the Hollywood Walk of Fame, and enter *The Guinness Book of Records* as history's longest-running film franchise.

Godzilla is, without a doubt, the King of the Monsters.

In this book, we will take you on a pictorial journey film by film from Godzilla's birth in 1954's seminal *Gojira*, to Toho Studios' most recent animated Godzilla adventures, as well as its many appearances in television, comics, and more.

This book is divided up by Era, beginning with the Showa Era in the 1950s, 60s, and 70s, up until the current Reiwa Era, which extends to the present day. The Godzilla film franchise is categorized by these eras, named after the Emperor who was in power in Japan at the time those films were made. The flavor and tone of the films in these eras also differ in interesting ways, and so we'll explore what evolves tonally from era to era, and how Godzilla as a character grows and changes from film to film.

And most important of all: the pictures that will take us on this journey. Toho Studios – the legendary film studio that created Godzilla – has given us unprecedented access to their entire official image library. In this book you will find never-before-seen stills, behind-the-scenes photos, concept art, and more, all beautifully realized in sumptuous full color and dramatic black and white.

Whether you've loved these films your whole life, or are completely new to the world of kaiju, this book will be a fascinating and comprehensive look at one of the world's most important and successful film franchises.

So without further ado... do you hear that thunderous footstep in the distance? Can you hear the ocean waves roiling into a maelstrom? And then, the mistakeable ear-splitting roar?

Welcome to the domain of the King of the Monsters: Godzilla.

昭和シリーズ

THE SHOWA ERA

The Showa Era of Godzilla films ran from 1954's original *Gojira* until *Terror of Mechagodzilla* in 1975. This run of 15 films would set the tone for all the movies that followed. They introduced Godzilla as a deadly and terrifying force of nature, evolving into a role of protector – and even friend – of humanity. They also introduced the world to a number of Godzilla's most famous foes and allies – King Ghidorah, Anguirus and Mechagodzilla to name a few – who would appear in numerous films throughout the franchise. Mothra and Rodan had already starred in their own movies before sharing the screen with Godzilla. This era is largely defined by a tone of whimsical fun, with huge monster battles and outlandish sci-fi and fantasy subplots. They're fun for the whole family, and are some of the most iconic examples of Godzilla and what these films represent to so many.

But before the aliens, robots, and undersea cultists entered the scene, there was the horrifying original film that started it all...

THE SHOWA ERA FILMS ARE:

GOJIRA • GODZILLA RAIDS AGAIN • KING KONG VS. GODZILLA
MOTHRA VS. GODZILLA • GHIDORAH, THE THREE-HEADED MONSTER
INVASION OF ASTRO-MONSTER • EBIRAH, HORROR OF THE DEEP • SON OF GODZILLA
DESTROY ALL MONSTERS • ALL MONSTERS ATTACK • GODZILLA VS. HEDORAH
GODZILLA VS. GIGAN • GODZILLA VS. MEGALON • GODZILLA VS. MECHAGODZILLA
TERROR OF MECHAGODZILLA

ゴジラ

GODZILLA 1954

DIRECTOR : ISHIRO HONDA
WRITTEN BY : TAKEO MURATA, ISHIRO HONDA
PRODUCED BY : TOMOYUKI TANAKA
SPECIAL EFFECTS DIRECTOR : EIJI TSUBURAYA
SCORE : AKIRA IFUKUBE
STARRING : AKIRA TAKARADA, MOMOKO KOCHI, TAKASHI SHIMURA, AKIHIKO HIRATA, HARUO NAKAJIMA

SILENCE. THEN, THUNDERING FOOTSTEPS. FINALLY, A DEAFENING, UNMISTAKEABLE ROAR, ACCOMPANIED BY STARK WHITE LETTERING OVER INKY BLACK: GODZILLA.

Thus begins one of the most influential and terrifying films ever made, Ishiro Honda's original masterpiece *Godzilla*. From this foreboding opening credits sequence we move to a boat, a fishing trawler, when its sailors are surprised by a blinding flash of light and some kind of horror emerging from the sea. This opening scene was directly inspired by the tragedy that befell the real-life Japanese fishing boat the *Daigo Fukuryu Maru* (aka the *Lucky Dragon 5*), whose crew earlier that same year suffered radiation poisoning after an American H-bomb test.

And all of this less than ten years after the atomic bombs were dropped on Hiroshima and Nagasaki. *Godzilla* is a film whose DNA is soaked with fear and reflection on how the nuclear age had devastated Japan. Its scenes of Tokyo set aflame by an invading force, of thousands fleeing their homes in fear, and of an unstoppable and indescribable menace would have been fresh in the minds of the Japanese public experiencing this film.

Godzilla begins – as described above – with the destruction of a Japanese fishing boat. Another boat is sent to investigate and it, too, is destroyed, its lone survivor bringing back a far-fetched tale of a sea creature destroying the ship. Soon, the villagers realize why the fishing has been so bad lately: the ancient sea monster known as Godzilla.

Godzilla finally surfaces and destroys the village on Odo Island, but director Ishiro Honda makes us wait almost 20 minutes to actually see the titular monster. The suspense is worth it, because soon Godzilla is revealed in all its horrifying glory.

Toho Studios truly put together a dream team to create this film. Starring as the chief scientist in charge of studying Godzilla – Dr. Yamane – is legendary actor Takashi Shimura, known for iconic roles in Kurosawa's *Seven Samurai*, *Rashomon*, and *Ikiru*. In the film, his daughter is caught between two loves: the eccentric eyepatch-wearing scientist Dr. Serizawa (Akihiko Hirata) and her new flame, handsome fisherman Hideto Ogata, played by Akira Takarada. Dr. Yamane longs for peace, and to study Godzilla due to its incredible age and resistance to radiation. The government, however, wants to destroy it. And the only weapon appears to be Serizawa's Oxygen Destroyer, which will destroy all life in Tokyo Bay.

Godzilla's plot may be relatively simple, but director Ishiro Honda makes sure we care about the people who are about to be killed. We meet a group of commuters annoyed at the delays on the subway. Minutes later, they meet their end when Godzilla emerges from the sea. A mother comforts her two young children, telling them they'll soon be with their father, who'd perished during the Second World War.

This film does not pull punches.

Speaking of the dream team Toho assembled, in addition to the all-star cast and visionary director Ishiro Honda, a slew of other artists contributed some of their very best work to this film: Eiji Tsuburaya oversaw the special effects, which included the famous suit, the miniatures, the matte paintings, the animation of Godzilla's atomic breath... everything. His work was revolutionary and at the time was truly cutting edge.

Actor Haruo Nakajima played Godzilla in the suit, bringing his athleticism and martial arts background into the character. He also went so far as to study bears at the local zoo for inspiration, and even incorporated elements of classic Japanese Noh Theatre. His performance made Godzilla anything but "just a guy in a suit".

Special consideration must also be given to the film's composer, the great Akira Ifukube. His score is instantly iconic, the lumbering, driving theme pushing ever forward, unceasing like the monster it represents. Ifukube's *Godzilla* theme is instantly recognizable, and like John Williams' theme for *Jaws* decades later, would become as much a part of Godzilla's identity as its heat ray or thunderous roar.

水爆大怪獣映画
ゴジラ
放射能を吐く大怪獣の暴威は日本全土を恐怖のドン底に叩き込んだ!
原作・香山滋
宝田明
河内桃子
平田昭彦
志村喬
東宝
東宝株式会社 製作・配給

GODZILLA, KING OF THE MONSTERS! (1956)

Two years after the release of *Godzilla* in Japan, American producers purchased the rights to distribute the film in the United States, on the condition that they would be able to dub the film in English, as well as providing for alterations that would make it more palatable for American audiences. The result is a film that is almost completely different from the original, with over half the film including new scenes with actor Raymond Burr playing a news reporter who has been inserted into scenes from the original film, commenting on the action and experiencing the tragic events from an American perspective. The film was a huge success and is the reason an international audience learned about Godzilla in the first place. Not until 2004 was the original film even available to American audiences, so for many, this is the Godzilla that started it all.

Opposite: One of the most iconic stills from the first film; Godzilla stares down the military.

Above: Godzilla destroying Tokyo's National Diet Building.

GODZILLA OR GOJIRA?

There's a lot of debate about the title of the original film in the series. Is it *Godzilla*? Or is the more accurate title *Gojira*, based on the Japanese lettering in the film?

The answer is somewhere in the middle. Translating Japanese to English is difficult for a number of reasons, not least of which being that Japanese has certain phonetic sounds that differ slightly from the English equivalent. As such, certain translations of the original title would read the three Japanese letters as "Go", "Ji", and "Ra". However, that middle letter can often be translated not as "Ji", but as "Zi". Same with the final letter, since Japanese speakers would pronounce an R sound as an L, that final letter might be pronounced as "La". So, just as much as it's "Gojira", the title of the film and name of the creature is also "Godzilla". Yes, it's a bit of a western mispronunciation, but it's also one that Toho themselves recommended as the English translation of the word. Therefore, for the purposes of this book, whenever we refer to the title of the 1954 original film, or for that matter of the character itself, we will use "Godzilla".

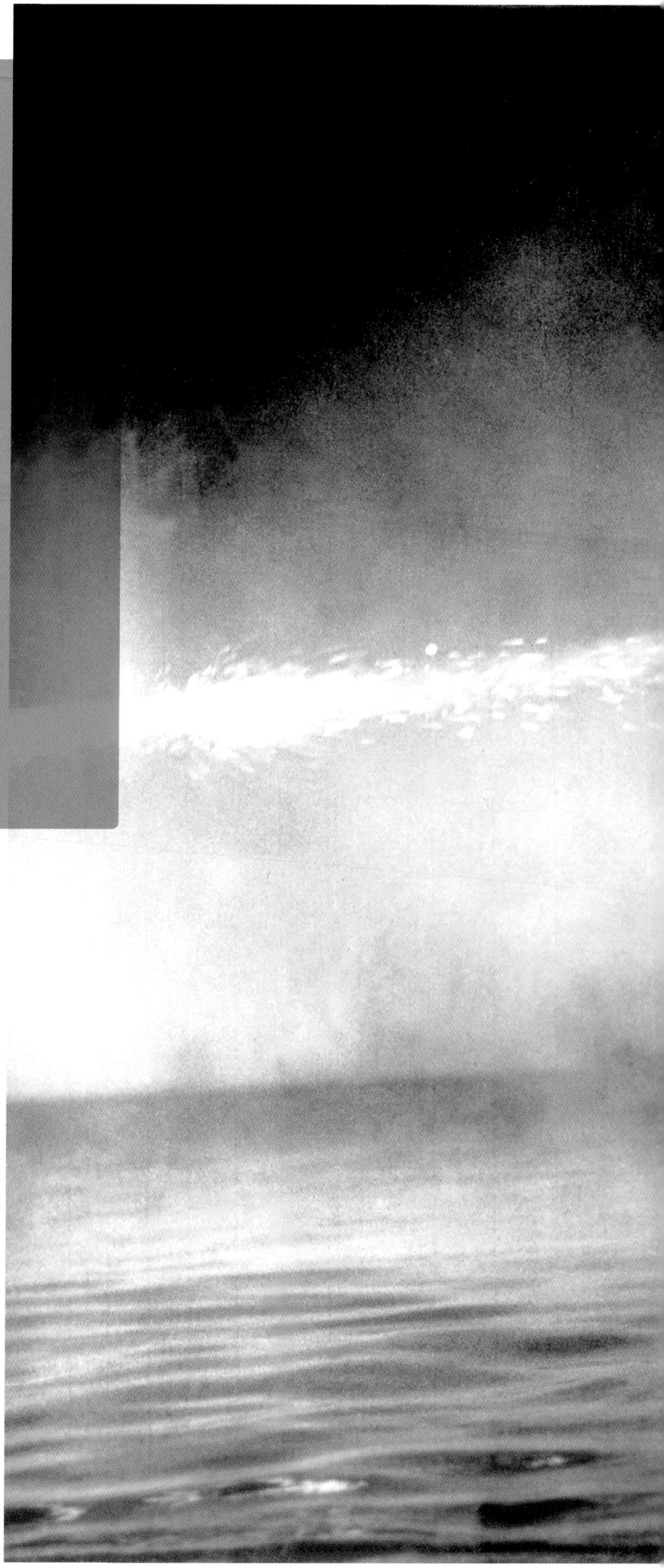

Above/Right: Godzilla under fire.

92

カメラ
永ミルクキャラ

Godzilla is a film about many things: fear of the atomic bomb, trauma from the horrors of the Second World War, a mourning of those lost to the tragedies at Hiroshima and Nagasaki, and a very real struggle with the atrocities endured, while accepting responsibility for the atrocities committed.

Something interesting happens when people watch *Godzilla* – they relate just as much to the monster as they do to the humans it kills. Godzilla is a force of nature, an innocent bystander, in a lot of ways, to mankind's penchant for destruction. We wake it up with the H-bomb, we anger it by attacking it… we must accept the consequences. When we ultimately destroy it, there is sadness that we had to use our own destructive nature to end the life of such a special creature.

Ishiro Honda's film paved the way for history's longest-running film franchise, which would evolve from a stark and sober examination of the horrors of the atomic age into family-friendly giant monster brawls complete with musical numbers, dance sequences, and even Hanna-Barbera cartoons. All of those are wonderful in and of themselves, and we'll get to them shortly! But first we must pay homage to the film that started it all, a film that without the artistry of the team that made it, could have easily disappeared into the sea of "irradiated monster movies" that would follow. Instead, the world got a layered and complex allegory for the atomic bomb and perhaps the most iconic monster cinema has ever known.

Opposite: Promotional photo of Godzilla unleashing its iconic heat ray.

Above: Godzilla battling both ground and air forces.

THE ITALIAN COLORIZED GODZILLA (AKA COZILLA)

In 1977, Italian horror and sci-fi director Luigi Cozzi released a re-edited and colorized version of *Godzilla*, featuring an all-new synth score by frequent Lucio Fulci collaborator Fabio Frizzi. This version of the film uses footage from the original Japanese cut, as well as the American edit, and now opens with stock footage of the bombing of Hiroshima and Nagasaki. The film has been colorized here, with red, yellow, and green tints placed over the footage, giving the whole experience a unique, psychedelic quality. This is an interesting oddity in the legacy of *Godzilla*, and is testament to the King of the Monsters' influence around the world.

Above: Promotional Material of Godzilla succumbing to the Oxygen Destroyer.

Right: Special Effects Director Eiji Tsuburaya with Haruo Nakajima in Godzilla suit.

Overleaf (left): Akira Takarada (left) and Akihiko Hirata as Hideto Ogata and Dr. Serizawa, about to unleash the Oxygen Destroyer.

Overleaf (right): Godzilla before a fiery Tokyo.

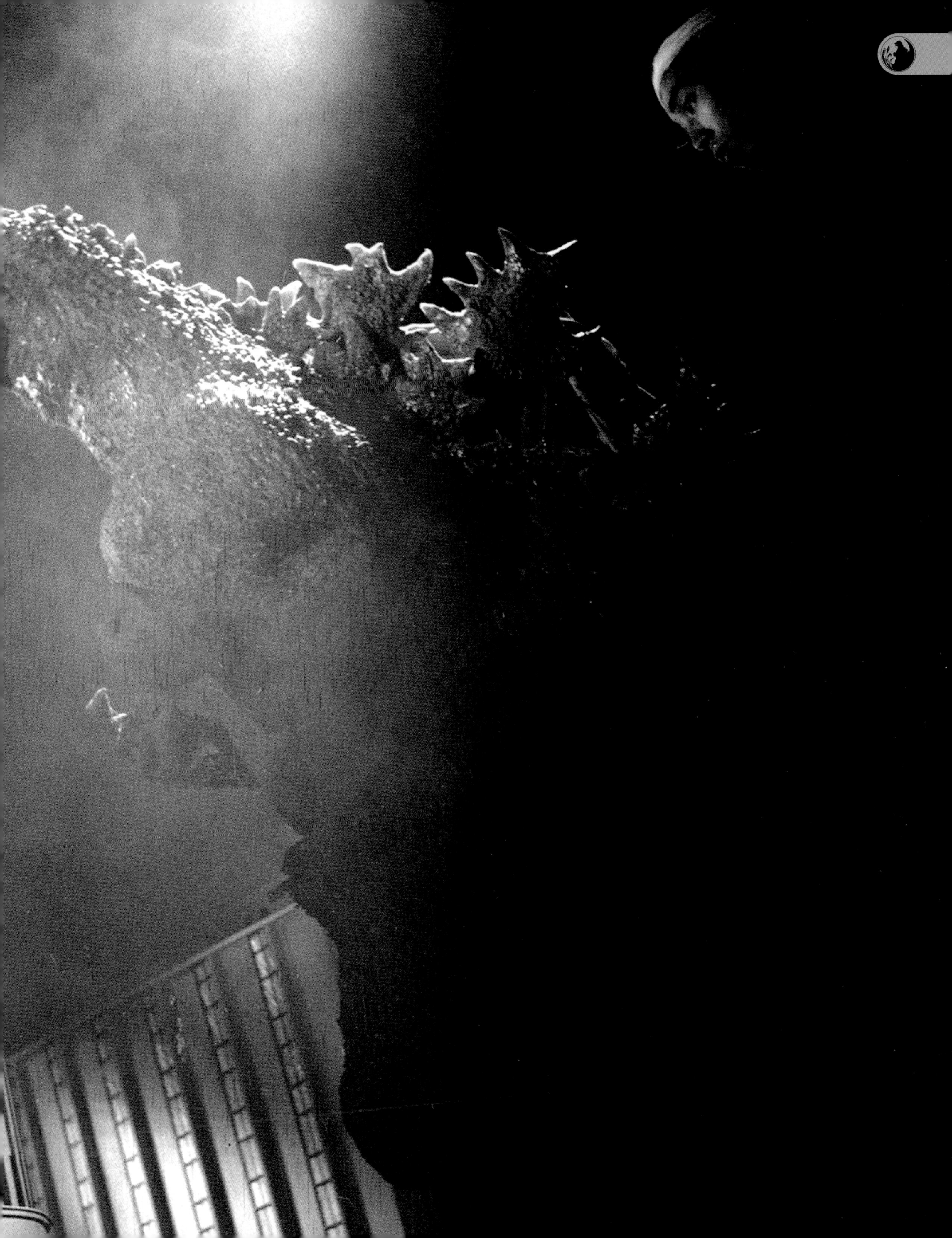

ゴジラの逆襲

GODZILLA RAIDS AGAIN (1955)

DIRECTOR : MOTOYOSHI ODA
WRITTEN BY : TAKEO MURATA, SHIGEAKI HIDAKA
PRODUCED BY : TOMOYUKI TANAKA
SPECIAL EFFECTS DIRECTOR : EIJI TSUBURAYA
SCORE : MASARU SATO
STARRING : HIROSHI KOIZUMI, SETSUKO WAKAYAMA, TAKASHI SHIMURA, MINORU CHIAKI, HARUO NAKAJIMA

FOLLOWING THE TREMENDOUS SUCCESS OF *GODZILLA* THE PREVIOUS YEAR, TOHO STUDIOS WANTED TO QUICKLY FOLLOW UP WITH A SEQUEL. AND SO, GODZILLA WAS RESURRECTED THE NEXT YEAR IN *GODZILLA RAIDS AGAIN*.

Due to Ishiro Honda being unavailable while working on another film, Toho turned to reliable horror director Motoyoshi Oda to bring Godzilla back to the screen for the second time.

In this film, we open with a pair of pilots surveying for fishing boats. One of them encounters engine trouble and crash lands on a nearby island, forcing the other to land to provide assistance. The two pilots soon find themselves witness to an epic and unexpected sight: a battle between two gargantuan monsters! Godzilla appears to be alive, and is in fact fighting Anguirus, an ancient dinosaur that nimbly maneuvers on all fours with a spiny shell covering its back.

Scientists – including Takashi Shimura reprising his role from the previous film – determine that this is another Godzilla, who, along with Anguirus, was also awoken by the H-bomb that roused the first film's Godzilla. They also correctly identify Anguirus, noting that its species is known for being extremely aggressive and dangerous, a natural foe to Godzilla.

The scientists note that Godzilla is again approaching the mainland. They attempt to use flares to lure it away from civilization, but those same flares draw Anguirus, prompting more fights, which are the hallmark of this film.

Director Motoyoshi Oda not only provides massive monster battles – the first time Godzilla would face off against other Kaiju (the Japanese term for giant monsters) – but also an engaging love story and a tale of two best friends whose lives are torn apart by the rampaging beasts.

Haruo Nakajima returned to portray Godzilla. He faced off against actor Katsumi Tezuka (also credited as occasionally playing Godzilla in the first film) who plays Anguirus. One interesting 'happy accident' that occurred while filming this movie involved the slow motion sequences. In making movies, film has to be shot at a high frame rate in order to be presented in slow motion later. Essentially, when you shoot something at, say, 60 frames per second (as opposed to the standard 24 frames per second), the film, when slowed down, will be fluid and look properly slow motion. This is the technique Honda used on the original *Godzilla* in order to give the beast a more massive, lumbering, epic appearance.

On *Godzilla Raids Again*, however, one of the cameramen accidentally slowed down the frame rate while shooting several scenes intended to be slow motion, resulting in the monsters appearing even more nimble and quick than when the fights had been filmed. This mistake revolutionized how monster movies would be later filmed, with several different frame rates used for the fight scenes depending on the action desired.

Eiji Tsuburaya returned as special effects director, and here continued to refine his skills with the epic battles in and around Osaka. In addition to the suits – built with lighter materials this time around to allow the actors more freedom of movement – Tsuburaya crafted detailed hand puppets, as well as a massive miniature of Osaka Castle that would prove so hardy that the actors had a difficult time destroying it once constructed. Truly, Godzilla begins its evolution here, from the stoic and unstoppable terror of the first film, into the battle-hardened beast fighting other giant monsters that audiences have come to expect.

Interestingly, the US release changed the title to *Gigantis the Fire Monster*, assuming that American audiences would be more inclined to see a movie about a new monster rather than a sequel to *Godzilla*. The American version was heavily edited and featured an all-new score pulled from other popular sci-fi films from the 1950s.

The film culminates on a snowy island, with an epic finale that puts Godzilla on ice for the first time (this would go on to be a theme of sorts). Thanks to *Godzilla Raids Again*, the precedent was set for Godzilla to fight other giant monsters. And the next film, coming seven years later, would be the most anticipated clash of all...

怪獣ゴジラ対新登場の暴龍アンギラス
日本全土狭しと暴れ廻る驚天動地の巨篇！

小泉博
千秋実
若山セツ子
土屋嘉男
木匠マユリ
山本廉
清水将夫
志村喬

原作 香山滋
監督 小田基義
特技監督 円谷英二

ゴジラの逆襲

製作 田中友幸
脚本 村田武雄
日高繁明
撮影 遠藤精一
美術監督 北猛夫
美術 安倍輝明
特殊技術 渡辺明
向山宏
城田正雄
録音 宮崎正信
照明 大沼正喜
音楽 佐藤勝

東宝

東宝株式会社 製作・配給

Printed in Japan

Opposite: Godzilla battles Anguirus.

Above: Godzilla and Anguirus destroying the city.

Left: Anguirus prepares to pounce on his foe.

33.

Left: Promotional photo of Godzilla primed for its final battle with Anguirus.

Top: Anguirus roars.

Above (middle): Citizens fleeing the marauding kaiju.

Above: Anguirus leaping in vicious attack.

キングコング対ゴジラ

KING KONG VS. GODZILLA (1962)

DIRECTOR : ISHIRO HONDA
WRITTEN BY : SHIN'ICHI SEKIZAWA
PRODUCED BY : TOMOYUKI TANAKA
SPECIAL EFFECTS DIRECTOR : EIJI TSUBURAYA
SCORE : AKIRA IFUKUBE
STARRING : JAMES YAGI, TADAO TAKASHIMA, KENJI SAHARA, SHOICHI HIROSE, HARUO NAKAJIMA

IN 1962, A SCRIPT FROM AMERICA CALLED *KING KONG MEETS FRANKENSTEIN* LANDED IN THE HALLS OF TOHO, AND THE STUDIO KNEW HISTORY WAS ABOUT TO BE MADE.

They quickly rewrote it to replace Frankenstein's Monster with Godzilla, hoping to revive their hit franchise that had lain dormant for almost a decade.

It's no secret that a major inspiration for Godzilla originally was Merian C. Cooper's 1933 classic *King Kong*. The 1952 re-release of that film – and subsequent massive success – paved the way for *Godzilla* to get the green light in the first place. *Kong*'s beautiful stop-motion animation was also hugely inspirational to special effects director Eiji Tsuburaya, a lifelong Kong fan.

So, when the opportunity arose, Tsuburaya dropped every other production he had going to return to the realm of Godzilla. Also returning would be Godzilla's original director, Ishiro Honda, as well as original producer Tomoyuki Tanaka and Godzilla actor Haruo Nakajima. But *King Kong vs. Godzilla* would be far from their previous film's sober reflection on the atomic age and humanity's endless cycle of violence. Instead, Honda would choose to make a light-hearted satire of the Japanese television industry, while squaring off two of cinema's most iconic giant monsters in the fight to end all fights.

King Kong vs. Godzilla follows Mr. Tako, the head of a pharmaceutical company who is disappointed in sales and blames the lackluster performance of TV commercials and shows featuring his product. Upon hearing about a giant monster on a small, mysterious island, he has the idea to capture the monster and turn it into his company's new spokesperson (or, perhaps more accurately, *spokescreature*).

Meanwhile, an American nuclear submarine crashes into an iceberg, releasing Godzilla from its icy slumber, where the creature's been since the finale of *Godzilla Raids Again* in 1955!

Tako's team of adventurers encounters natives on Faro Island, and they find themselves besieged by a giant octopus that seeks to destroy the village. Soon, however, King Kong emerges from the jungle and destroys the octopus foe. Kong soon thereafter falls asleep after drinking some strange juice, as well as being lulled to sleep by the rhythmic drumming and singing of the native islanders, prompting Tako's team to strap him to a huge raft and tow the sleeping Kong back to Japan.

Eventually, Kong awakens and breaks free of his bonds, swimming ashore in Japan and immediately encountering Godzilla, who is in the midst of its own monster rampage. The two beasts begin to battle! Kong is powerful, but it is clear that he is no match for Godzilla's heat ray. As Kong retreats (and Tako desperately tries to concoct ways to recapture "his" monster), the army sets up another powerful electric fence (this time with 1,000,000 volts instead of the paltry 50,000 they'd previously tried in the original film), to deter Godzilla. And it works – until Kong arrives and absorbs the electrical energy, becoming exponentially more powerful.

With Kong now stronger than ever, the army has the idea of purposefully pitting Kong and Godzilla against one another, in the hope that Kong will finally destroy Godzilla once and for all. So, they lull the giant ape to sleep once again and, using a canopy of huge balloons, fly him to Mount Fuji and drop him next to Godzilla for one final fight.

And fight they do! A gargantuan brawl occurs, with both monsters gaining the upper hand from time to time. It's truly a spectacle, complete with a freak lightning storm, the destruction of a huge miniature of Osaka Castle, and a cataclysmic tumble into the ocean waves.

This film marked a vast departure from the previous two films in the series. Although *Godzilla Raids Again* had featured giant monsters fighting each other, the tone was still dramatic, and was intended for adults. Tsuburaya specifically wanted to shift the franchise to be more child-friendly and fun, steering the design and characterization of Godzilla and King Kong to be more anthropomorphic, and imbuing the fight scenes with humor. While Honda was not necessarily a fan

東宝

創立30周年
記念映画

キングコング対ゴジラ

KING KONG vs GODZILLA

ゴジラ勝つか?コング勝つか?全世界話題の大怪獣巨篇

総天然色

監督・本多猪四郎
特技監督・円谷英二
製作・田中友幸

高島忠夫
佐原健二
藤木悠
浜美枝
若林映子
田崎潤
松村達雄
平田昭彦
有島一郎

of this approach, Toho knew this was the right path for the future of the franchise, and so the new tone of the series evolved into its hallmark lightheartedness.

Of course, the US crafted its own dubbed version of the film, re-editing much of the movie and filming entirely new segments, just as it had done with *Godzilla* in 1954. In the American version, several newscasters comment on the events from afar, while Mr. Tako is almost entirely cut out of the movie, as it was feared his cartoonish performance would be deemed too silly by American audiences.

King Kong vs. Godzilla was a massive success, and sparked a flood of sequels that would become the longest consistent run of Godzilla films in the franchise. The Showa Era was about to really kick into high gear...

Opposite: Godzilla at Osaka Castle, about to battle King Kong one last time.

Above: King Kong about to grab Godzilla's tail.

KING KONG AND TOHO

Toho would have one more outing with King Kong, in 1967 with *King Kong Escapes*. Reuniting director Ishiro Honda with special effects director Eiji Tsuburaya, as well as *Godzilla* star Akira Takarada, this co-production with animation legends Rankin/Bass would see Kong under mind control by the nefarious Dr Who (no relation to the BBC Time Lord). Throughout the film, Kong battles against a number of monsters, including Mechani-Kong and Gorosaurus. A tonal departure from the rest of the *Kong* franchise, *King Kong Escapes* captures the childlike joy that was the hallmark of its *Godzilla* franchise cousins.

Top: Godzilla's far more concerned with its foe than with the circling helicopter.

Left: Godzilla's fighting stance.

Above: Kenji Sahara (left) and Mie Hama fleeing Godzilla.

Opposite: Godzilla's famous heat ray.

モスラ対ゴジラ

MOTHRA VS. GODZILLA (1964)

DIRECTOR : ISHIRO HONDA
WRITTEN BY : SHIN'ICHI SEKIZAWA
PRODUCED BY : TOMOYUKI TANAKA
SPECIAL EFFECTS DIRECTOR : EIJI TSUBURAYA
SCORE : AKIRA IFUKUBE
STARRING : AKIRA TAKARADA, YURIKO HOSHI, HIROSHI KOIZUMI, THE PEANUTS, HARUO NAKAJIMA

AFTER THE ENORMOUS SUCCESS OF *KING KONG VS. GODZILLA*, TOHO BROUGHT THE TEAM BACK TOGETHER FOR ANOTHER GIANT MONSTER MASH-UP WITH *MOTHRA VS. GODZILLA*.

Mothra, the insect god from Infant Island, was chosen as Godzilla's nemesis after her own film *Mothra* in 1961 proved wildly popular. She would go on to become one of the *Godzilla* franchise's most popular kaiju, as well as starring in her own series of films. This would also be the final time in the Showa Era where Godzilla is the main antagonist of the film.

In *Mothra vs. Godzilla*, a mysterious giant egg washes ashore, quickly garnering curiosity as to its origins, as well as arguments over its ownership. Due to the fact it had been found in a village's fishing waters, it is sold by the villagers to Happy Enterprises, a conglomerate that seeks to turn it into the star attraction of a new theme park.

Meanwhile, a pair of tiny twin women – known as the *Shobijin*, and played by popular pop duo The Peanuts – appear saying they are from Mothra's home of Infant Island, and that the egg belongs to Mothra. They ask for its return. They also warn that when the egg hatches, the larva will be large, powerful, and dangerous. Of course, the businessmen think only of profit, and not only ignore their warnings but attempt to capture and exploit the magical twins as well!

The Shobijin seek the help of a trio of reporters, who empathize with their plight and attempt to help through broadcasting news reports urging public sympathy for Mothra, but sadly, profit and greed win the day. The twins return to Infant Island, having been rejected by the humans of Japan.

But soon... Godzilla appears! Having apparently been buried in mud since its battle with King Kong, it is awoken by a radioactive fragment and begins another rampage of destruction across Japan. With no way to stop the devastating attack, the trio of reporters travel to Infant Island to beg Mothra to forgive humanity's rebuttal of her request to return her egg, and help them battle Godzilla and save Japan.

At first, all seems lost as the islanders who worship Mothra flatly refuse. After all, why would they – or their deity – help mankind when mankind refused to help them? But Mothra herself agrees, and flies to Japan to take on Godzilla!

And that battle is spectacular. Mothra's wings are as deadly as they are beautiful, generating hurricane force winds that batter Godzilla into submission. Godzilla attempts to destroy her egg, but the maternal Mothra will stop at nothing to protect her young. She fights with every ounce she has, even to the point of sacrificing her own life. We learn from the Shobijin that she is at the end of her lifecycle.

Godzilla appears the victor, and it seems nothing can stop it from destroying Japan completely. Until...

The egg hatches...

And *two* giant larvae emerge! Mothra has had twins! The larvae attack Godzilla and show that size doesn't necessarily matter when it comes to kaiju. The infant monsters band together and use their ability to spray silk from their mandibles to subdue Godzilla and send it retreating into the sea. As the larvae return to Infant Island, the Shobijin tell us that Mothra will live again through her children, and our human heroes reflect that perhaps what we can take away from this experience is that we have to trust each other if we are going to overcome our common foes.

"MOTHRA'S WINGS ARE AS DEADLY AS THEY ARE BEAUTIFUL, GENERATING HURRICANE FORCE WINDS THAT BATTER GODZILLA INTO SUBMISSION."

東宝

マッハ3の巨蛾か！ミサイル重戦車の
ゴジラか！空・海・陸を揺がす世紀の激斗

総天然色

モスラ対ゴジラ

GODZILLA AGAINST MOTHRA

宝田明
星由里子
ザ・ピーナッツ
伊藤エミ
伊藤ユミ
小泉博
藤木悠
佐原健二
田島義文
小杉義男
藤田進
田崎潤

監督 本多猪四郎
特技監督 円谷英二
製作 田中友幸
脚本 関沢新一

The shadow of nuclear war hangs over this film, with Honda portraying Infant Island as a wasteland after repeated H-bomb tests, with only a small oasis left for Mothra and her followers. There is also the spectre of guilt, with the kind, nurturing god Mothra helping humanity despite the fact that mankind has not only destroyed her island but also spurned her pleas for help.

Another theme of the film is that of unending greed. The corporate executives prove to be as much of a monster in this film as Godzilla, with Honda portraying their demise as purely due to their own avarice. The fact that Godzilla is merely the method of their death, but that the circumstances placing them where they would be in harm's way are solely due to their own choices, is a clear commentary about how the acquisition of wealth regularly takes control of our lives, perhaps at the cost of actually living.

Yet again, Honda's vision for giant monster movies transcends the childlike fun of watching two kaiju duke it out. His unique blend of youthful wonder and glee, with complex social commentary, is a driving force of the Showa Era, and continues on as Godzilla transitions from being a menace... to a savior.

Above: Mothra - protective of her egg - attacks Godzilla from the skies.

Right: Godzilla rises from its slumber under the sand.

Opposite (above): Mothra about to take flight.

Opposite (below): Mothra's twin larvae on the war path.

Above: Mothra coming to protect her egg.

Left: Promotional image of Godzilla battling Mothra's larvae.

Opposite: Promotional still of Godzilla having a very tough go of it against Mothra.

Top: Godzilla ruining yet another priceless structure.

Above: Promotional artwork of Godzilla and Mothra in battle.

Right: Godzilla versus its oldest foe: power lines!

三大怪獣 地球最大の決戦

GHIDORAH, THE THREE-HEADED MONSTER (1964)

DIRECTOR : ISHIRO HONDA
WRITTEN BY : SHIN'ICHI SEKIZAWA
PRODUCED BY : TOMOYUKI TANAKA
SPECIAL EFFECTS DIRECTOR : EIJI TSUBURAYA
SCORE : AKIRA IFUKUBE
STARRING : YOSUKE NATSUKI, YURIKO HOSHI, AKIKO WAKABAYASHI, THE PEANUTS, HARUO NAKAJIMA

WHEN ONE OF TOHO'S FILMS FELL THROUGH, LEAVING THE POPULAR NEW YEAR SLOT SUDDENLY OPEN, THEY KNEW EXACTLY WHO COULD FILL IT: THE KING OF THE MONSTERS!

Ghidorah, the Three-Headed Monster was rushed into production in order to come out by the end of the year, making 1964 a year with two Godzilla films! This movie would see not only the return of Godzilla (played again by Haruo Nakajima), but also Mothra (in larval form), as well as another monster from a hit Toho film, the pterodactyl-like Rodan. Decades before Marvel would concoct the Marvel Cinematic Universe, Toho was making their own MCU: a Monster Cinematic Universe.

The villain this time would be King Ghidorah, a massive, golden, winged, three-headed beast from space. The threat would be so great that for the first time, Godzilla would turn from a peril to mankind to being a protector.

The story of *Ghidorah, the Three-Headed Monster* begins with news that a princess from a foreign land is traveling to Japan seeking asylum from those who wish to assassinate her. Moments before her private jet explodes, a voice from space speaks to her telling her to flee, and so the princess leaps from the plane into the night sky. The jet is destroyed, and the princess is presumed dead.

Meanwhile, meteorites have been falling from space at an alarming rate, and one meteorite is not only glowing but appears to be growing larger by the day.

Soon, the princess reappears dressed in the clothes of a vagabond and claiming to be a prophet from the planet Venus. She preaches to throngs of people that a great calamity is coming to Earth, and she has come to warn us about the threat. Of course, no one really believes her, and her would-be assassins are still hot on her trail.

Godzilla emerges from the sea, and Rodan – a massive, irradiated pteranodon – bursts forth from a volcano. Both begin wreaking havoc as they battle each other. Shortly afterward, King Ghidorah hatches from the fallen meteorite, a fiery paragon of death and destruction.

Once scientists realize that the princess has been possessed by Venusian spirits, they believe her dark prophecies of King Ghidorah. They appeal to the Shobijin of Infant Island for help from Mothra, who is still in larval form, as one of the two twin larvae has perished, apparently. She obliges. But convincing Godzilla and Rodan to put aside their differences and join forces against King Ghidorah is a tall order. A fascinating scene ensues where Mothra actually speaks (in monster language, translated for us by the Shobijin) to Godzilla and Rodan in an attempt to reason with them, to convince them to team up against their common foe.

Left: The introduction of Ghidorah's Gravity Beams

東宝

夏木陽介
星由里子
若林映子
小泉博
ザ・ピーナッツ
伊藤エミ
伊藤ユミ
伊藤久哉
佐原健二
平田昭彦
志村喬

ラドン
キングギドラ
キングギドラ
ゴジラ
モスラ

総天然色
三大怪獣
地球最大の決戦

監督 本多猪四郎
特技監督 円谷英二
製作 田中友幸
脚本 関沢新一

Meanwhile, King Ghidorah rains mayhem on the world, its three evil heads spewing Gravity Beams that can level cities and prove a formidable threat to the other kaiju. Mothra fails to convince Godzilla and Rodan to fight with her and bravely tries to take on the beast on her own, but when King Ghidorah proves too powerful, and Godzilla and Rodan witness this, the unthinkable happens. They become friends, and battle together with Mothra in order to defeat this monster from space.

The battle is indeed huge and epic, and is masterfully intercut with the culmination of the story with the possessed princess and her assassins. *Ghidorah, the Three-Headed Monster* is another example of why director Ishiro Honda's work is so enduring and effective: we care about the monsters fighting because we care about the people caught in the middle. In addition, tremendous care is given to the monsters themselves, in this film becoming not only human enough to talk to one another, but blending masterful puppetry and stunt work to accomplish some truly remarkable big monster fights.

Above: Behind the Scenes photo of Ghidorah (Shoichi Hirose) about to do battle.

Right: The debut of Rodan to the Godzilla universe.

Opposite (above): Godzilla emerges from the sea.

Opposite (below): Rodan soars into action.

Above: Behind the scenes photo of King Ghidorah.

Left: Mothra's larva hears the call.

Opposite: Four titans meet for the first time.

Tsuburaya's special effects work here was some of the best of his career, constructing a massive miniature of Mount Fuji that reportedly took 12,000 hours to build, and having to use a synchronous combination of stunt person, puppetry, and wire-work to bring King Ghidorah to life.

Most importantly, this film would have a monster-sized impact on the trajectory of the Godzilla franchise. Godzilla has by now transitioned from being an enemy of the human race to being its savior. The movie has also proven that audiences love seeing Godzilla go toe to toe with other monsters in the cinematic arena.

Godzilla will go on to face many new foes over the course of its lifetime, but King Ghidorah proved too irresistible a menace to leave behind just yet.

Left: The huge final monster brawl, as seen in an early publicity still

Top: King Ghidorah's Gravity Beams.

Above: Godzilla and Rodan in battle.

怪獣大戦争

INVASION OF ASTRO-MONSTER (1965)

DIRECTOR : ISHIRO HONDA
WRITTEN BY : SHIN'ICHI SEKIZAWA
PRODUCED BY : TOMOYUKI TANAKA
SPECIAL EFFECTS DIRECTOR : EIJI TSUBURAYA
SCORE : AKIRA IFUKUBE
STARRING : NICK ADAMS, AKIRA TAKARADA, JUN TAZAKI, YOSHIO TSUCHIYA, HARUO NAKAJIMA, KUMI MIZUNO

WITH GODZILLA MORE POPULAR THAN EVER, ANOTHER SEQUEL WAS QUICKLY IN THE WORKS, THIS TIME A CO-PRODUCTION WITH AMERICAN ANIMATION COMPANY UPA.

For the first time in the Godzilla series, we are introduced directly to space aliens. Specifically, we first encounter Godzilla franchise mainstays, the devious Xiliens.

We're thrown right into the action, with a Japanese and an American astronaut flying from Earth to the mysterious new Planet X, recently discovered hidden in our solar system. To their surprise, when they arrive on Planet X they are urged into the secret underground base of the inhabitants of Planet X, the Xiliens, who all work at the bidding of their computerized leader, the Controller.

The Xiliens explain that their planet is plagued by a horrible creature known as Monster Zero, whose presence has turned their planet's surface into a wasteland and has forced them to live underground. Soon, when Monster Zero appears and begins to wreak havoc on the surface (no doubt awoken by the arrival of the Earthling rocket), the astronauts recognize it immediately. They know it by a different name, however: King Ghidorah.

It appears King Ghidorah fled Earth entirely after losing to Godzilla, Rodan, and Mothra in the previous film, and has turned its rage toward Planet X. The Xiliens make a request of the astronauts: may they borrow Godzilla and Rodan from Earth in order to battle King Ghidorah once again? In return for this exchange, they offer Earth a staggering prize: the cure for cancer.

Despite misgivings on the part of the astronauts, Earth agrees to this exchange, and the Xiliens transport a sleeping Godzilla and Rodan to Planet X. Meanwhile, the American astronaut Glenn has begun dating a mysterious young woman, and the Japanese astronaut Fuji (played here by Godzilla regular Akira Takarada) is attempting to convince his sister not to date the strange inventor Tetsuo.

Eventually, Tetsuo stumbles upon a Xilien secret and is captured by Xilien spies on Earth!

Fuji and Glenn return to Planet X to witness the battle between the monsters, and are not disappointed. Godzilla and Rodan handily defeat King Ghidorah in battle and, as thanks, the Xiliens gift them a recording that will share the cure for cancer as promised. They go back to Earth, but not before encountering something truly bizarre: there are exact copies of Glenn's new girlfriend here on Planet X!

Upon returning to Earth, the Xiliens' inevitable double-cross is revealed: they do not have the cure for cancer, and instead have used mind control to take ownership over King Ghidorah, Godzilla, and Rodan. They will use them to destroy the Earth if we do not surrender.

Glenn confronts his girlfriend who reveals herself to be a Xilien spy, but also admits she has fallen in love with him and wants him to surrender so they can live together as Xiliens. Unfortunately, love is illegal on Planet X and she is summarily executed by her people.

Soon, the astronauts discover that one of Tetsuo's inventions can be used to destroy the Xilien threat and release the kaiju from their mind control, which helps the efforts of Earth to not be taken over by the aliens, but also gives the monsters free reign to fight and destroy as they will. A gigantic monster battle ensues and soon Godzilla and Rodan disappear into the sea while Ghidorah escapes once more into space.

This film is a true space opera, and although it was marred by budgetary restraints and more disagreements over how childlike and lighthearted the monsters should be, the result is a blast of a sci-fi motion picture. It set the stage for future Godzilla instalments that would continue to lean heavily into science fiction, space aliens, and space travel – all elements that would later become hallmarks of the franchise.

Once again, the original team is back together, by now working seamlessly with one another and perfecting the challenging special effects on a low budget with very little time. Their creativity also continued to develop, with an entirely new language created for the Xiliens that was a combination of bizarre hand gestures and French and German dialects.

東宝
総天然色
怪獣大戦争
宇宙の帝王X星をゆるがすゴジラ・ラドン・キングギドラの大激闘！
監督・本多猪四郎
製作・田中友幸
脚本・関沢新一
東宝製作・配給
宝田明
ニック・アダムス
水野久美
沢井桂子
久保明
土屋嘉男
田崎潤
田島義文
田武謙三
村上冬樹
清水元
千石規子
佐々木孝丸
INVASION OF ASTRO-MONSTER

The partnership with UPA also resulted in the casting of American actor Nick Adams as the astronaut Glenn, as well as encouraging the filmmakers to jump right into the action, as opposed to starting with a lot of exposition. This, they felt, would be more appealing to American audiences, and it would be partly through UPA's involvement in this and in releasing future Godzilla films that would see the Godzilla franchise become even more of a phenomenon in the US.

Another sequel was in the works immediately, this time introducing a whole new monster for Godzilla to battle...

Left: A reunion of three foes on the moon-like Planet X.

Above: Behind the scenes photo of the rocket miniature, with stage lights and the wooden set visible above and below.

Above: Behind the scenes photo of Rodan about to take flight.

Left: UFOs coming to take Godzilla to the moon Planet X.

Opposite (above): Monster Zero (aka King Ghidorah) decimating Planet X.

Opposite (below): The Xiliens' high-tech base.

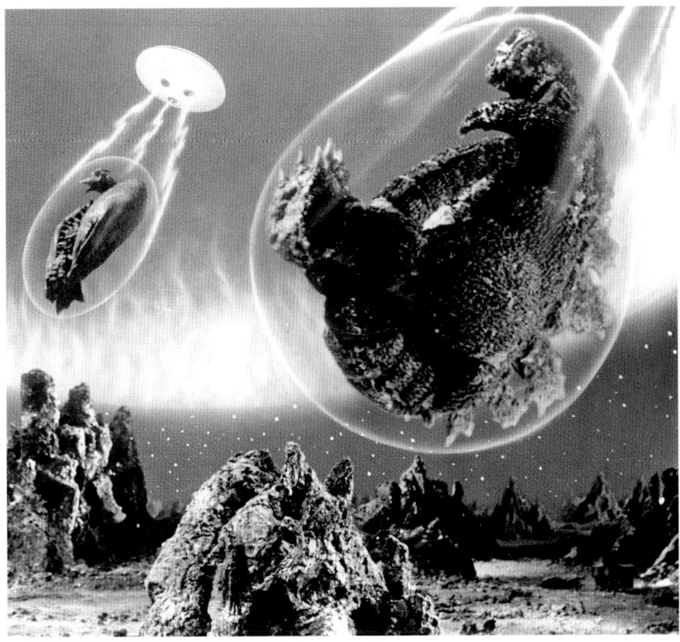

Opposite: Godzilla doing the now-iconic victory dance.

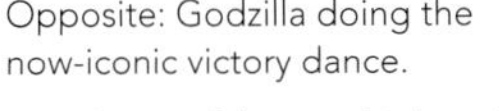

Top: Some of the new high-tech weaponry deployed by the military.

Above (right): Promotional art showing Godzilla and Rodan's transport to Planet X.

Above (left): Promotional art of the epic battle on Planet X, with Xiliens in front.

ゴジラ・エビラ・モスラ　南海の大決闘

EBIRAH, HORROR OF THE DEEP (1966)

DIRECTOR : JUN FUKUDA
WRITTEN BY : SHIN'ICHI SEKIZAWA
PRODUCED BY : TOMOYUKI TANAKA
SPECIAL EFFECTS DIRECTOR : EIJI TSUBURAYA
SCORE : MASARU SATO
STARRING : AKIRA TAKARADA, KUMI MIZUNO, CHOTARO TOGIN, AKIHIKO HIRATA, HARUO NAKAJIMA

IN 1966, GODZILLA RETURNS VIA ANOTHER REWRITE OF A PRE-EXISTING SCRIPT. ORIGINALLY, KING KONG WAS GOING TO RETURN TO THE BIG SCREEN IN A FILM WHERE THE GIANT APE BATTLED EBIRAH.

However, Toho knew that Godzilla was a better match for the aquatic menace, and rewrote the script to reflect that.

Budgetary restrictions famously hampered this production, which also saw a mostly new creative team at the helm. Replacing Ishiro Honda as director was Jun Fukuda, who would go on to make a number of Godzilla's most famous outings. Stepping in to fill the shoes of composer Akira Ifukube is Masaru Sato, returning after composing the music of *Godzilla Raids Again*. His score here shifts from the bombastic orchestral themes we've become used to in favor of 1960s surf rock, electric guitars jamming as giant crustacean claws rise from perilous waves.

The setting also shifts from mainland Japan to a remote island somewhere in the Pacific. This decision was largely made due to budgetary constraints: fewer cities means fewer miniature sets to be built and destroyed. The special effects were still overseen by Eiji Tsuburaya, supervising now as head of his own company, but the actual special effects director on set was newcomer Sadamasa Arikawa. Instead of the smooth experience of the previous films, with crews consistent and having gotten the process down to a well-oiled machine, *Ebirah* would prove a challenge to film. The outcome, however, is a unique entry in the *Godzilla* canon with some truly memorable moments.

In the film, we follow a group of stowaways on a luxury yacht as they get lost at sea during a horrible storm. Washing up on Letchi Island (a neighbor to Mothra's home, Infant Island), they immediately run afoul of the villainous group known as the Red Bamboo. We learn that Red Bamboo – a military organization (from nearby Devil's Island, of course, a fitting home for evildoers) is harvesting ingredients for an atomic bomb, and using the local villagers as slaves!

They also encounter the deadly Ebirah, a giant crustacean that lurks in the waters around Letchi Island. The Red Bamboo have concocted a strange yellow liquid that appears to drive Ebirah away, but any vessels without this yellow substance soon find themselves impaled on Ebirah's horrifying claws.

Soon, our heroes stumble upon a sleeping Godzilla (taking a much-needed nap since its battle with King Ghidorah), as well as a slumbering Mothra, who the islanders pray will awaken and save their enslaved brothers and sisters. Using a lightning rod, our heroes awaken Godzilla, who not only battles Ebirah (in a now-iconic boulder-throwing match) but also proceeds to wreak havoc on the Red Bamboo's military base.

Eventually, Mothra does indeed awaken, and battles between Godzilla, Mothra, and Ebirah culminate in a claw-ripping, explosive finale!

Ebirah, Horror of the Deep also gives us our most human-like Godzilla yet. Godzilla seems to notice the people in this film more than ever, their plights now seeming to be almost interesting to Godzilla, whereas they had been unnoticeable before, if not a specific target of destruction. There's even a sequence where it appears Godzilla is meditating. Tsuburaya's quest to humanize the kaiju was certainly becoming fruitful. And in Godzilla's next outing, we would get the character at its most comedic and paternal yet...

"USING A LIGHTNING ROD, OUR HEROES AWAKEN GODZILLA, WHO NOT ONLY BATTLES EBIRAH... BUT ALSO PROCEEDS TO WREAK HAVOC ON THE RED BAMBOO'S MILITARY BASE."

東宝

カラー作品

ゴジラ・エビラ・モスラ

南海の大決闘

凶悪新怪獣エビラ！陸・海・空に展開する三大怪獣世紀の対決！

監督・福田純

特技監督・円谷英二

製作 田中友幸

宝田明
水野久美
砂塚秀夫
当銀長太郎
伊吹徹
平田昭彦
ペア・バンビ
田崎潤

Opposite: Mothra returns to the franchise.

Left: Godzilla is ready to do battle with the angry crustacean.

Top: Godzilla and Ebirah finally meet.

Above: Mothra swoops into action.

Opposite: Godzilla is victorious once more.

怪獣島の決戦 ゴジラの息子

SON OF GODZILLA (1967)

DIRECTOR : JUN FUKUDA
WRITTEN BY : SHIN'ICHI SEKIZAWA, KAZUE SHIBA
PRODUCED BY : TOMOYUKI TANAKA
SPECIAL EFFECTS DIRECTOR : EIJI TSUBURAYA
SCORE : MASARU SATO
STARRING : TADAO TAKASHIMA, AKIRA KUBO, BEVERLY MAEDA, "LITTLE MAN" MACHAN, SEIJI ONAKA

MOST OF THE SAME CREW THAT WORKED ON *EBIRAH, HORROR OF THE DEEP*, RETURNED AS HONDA AND THE REST OF THE ORIGINAL *GODZILLA* TEAM WERE PREOCCUPIED MAKING TOHO'S OTHER KONG OUTING, *KING KONG ESCAPES*.

A Pacific island setting was chosen once again to help with budgetary constraints, but this time adding a crucial and beloved element: Godzilla's "son", Minilla.

The plot is relatively straightforward: a group of scientists are on Solgell Island testing a weather control device. Their hope is that if they can make this device work properly, then world hunger will be a thing of the past, as they'll be able to control the weather in places as inhospitable as the Sahara, or the Siberian Tundra. They test their invention, despite interruptions by two newcomers: one, a reporter from the mainland and the other a woman who has grown up alone in the wilds of the island. After a malfunction inadvertently causes a radioactive storm to ravage the island, knocking out most of their equipment, they are stranded! What's more, the praying mantises native to the island have been irradiated by the experiment and have grown to gargantuan size!

But then they discover the source of their malfunction: interference from the telepathic cries of an infant inside of an egg: a baby Godzilla.

The infant Godzilla – who is named Minilla – cries for help while under attack by the giant mantises (called Kamacuras), and we all know who answers that cry... Godzilla! The monster emerges from the ocean and not only saves the child, but adopts it and begins to teach it how to be a powerful kaiju, just like its father.

Toho wanted to appeal to not only a younger crowd with this Instalment, but most specifically to a 'date night' crowd, feeling that the adorable baby Godzilla would elicit sympathy from the young couples in the audience. Godzilla would also be its most human yet, taking the young kaiju under its proverbial wing and for the first time performing some genuine comedic slapstick as the iconic monster!

Godzilla's original (and up until now, essentially only) actor Haruo Nakajima returns yet again, but we also get a new performer to don the suit! They wanted Godzilla to appear significantly larger than Minilla, so a larger, heavier suit was constructed, one that was too large and unwieldy for Nakajima to use comfortably. So while he appears in only two scenes where his scale isn't as necessary, for much of the film actor Seji Onaka – himself a much larger performer – was the paternal Godzilla.

Playing the adorable Minilla is an actor called "Marchan the Dwarf", chosen specifically for his ability to display remarkable athleticism in such a constricting suit.

Several new monsters appear in the film, causing the characters to dub this island "Monster Island". There are the aforementioned Kamacuras, as well as the giant poisonous spider Kumonga. Special effects supervisor Sadamasa Arikawa had to use 20 puppeteers at a time to manipulate the enormous marionettes that played these gargantuan creatures.

Although certainly a massive departure from Godzilla's original terrifying introduction, *Son of Godzilla* not only humanized Godzilla further, but introduced a true sense of camp and humor that permeated much of the rest of the Showa Era. There's a sense of undeniable fun and affection for these characters on display throughout this film. Fukuda, Arikawa, and their team crafted a sweet adventure that ends on a heartfelt note of fatherly love and a son that just wants to make his father proud.

Despite the love between father and son, the Godzilla franchise was waning in popularity, and Toho wasn't sure that they could sustain it much longer. So, a plan was hatched to end the series on a high note, bringing back the original creative team and every single monster for one last blockbuster monster brawl...

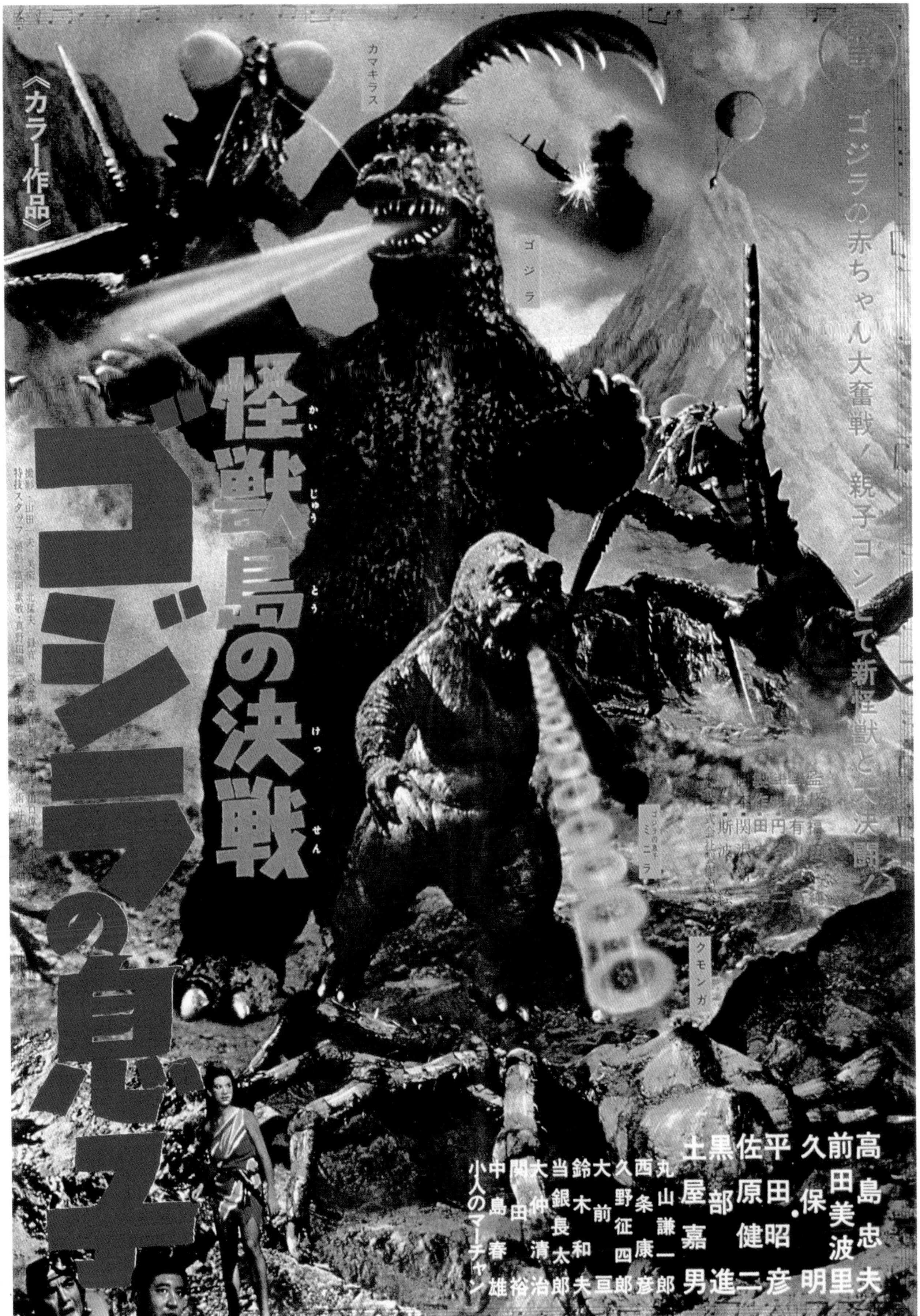
《カラー作品》
カマキラス
ゴジラ
ゴジラの赤ちゃん大奮戦／親子コン…で新怪獣と大決闘／
怪獣島の決戦
かい じゅう とう けっ せん
ゴジラの息子
ゴジラの息子 ミニラ
クモンガ
高島忠夫
前田美波里
久保明
平田昭彦
佐原健二
黒部進
土屋嘉男
丸山謙一郎
西条康彦
久野征四郎
大前亘
鈴木和夫
当銀長太郎
大仲清治
関田裕
中島春雄
小人のマーチャン

Top: The deadly Kamacuras.

Above: Minilla, so young and innocent.

Right: Minilla doing a victory dance.

Opposite: Minilla very much out of its element against a Kamacura.

Right: Kamacuras attacking the research station.

Opposite: Promotional artwork of Godzilla and Minilla unleashing their Heat Rays.

Above: Godzilla saves Minilla from Kumonga.

Right: Kamacuras about to strike!

怪獣総進撃

DESTROY ALL MONSTERS (1968)

DIRECTOR : ISHIRO HONDA
WRITTEN BY : ISHIRO HONDA, TAKESHI KIMURA
PRODUCED BY : TOMOYUKI TANAKA
SPECIAL EFFECTS DIRECTOR : EIJI TSUBURAYA
SCORE : AKIRA IFUKUBE
STARRING : AKIRA KUBO, JUN TAZAKI, YUKIKO KOBAYASHI, YOSHIO TSUCHIYA, HARUO NAKAJIMA

WITH AN UNCERTAIN FUTURE FOR THE GODZILLA FRANCHISE, TOHO BROUGHT BACK MUCH OF THE ORIGINAL TEAM FOR ONE FINAL EXPLOSIVE MATCH-UP, A GODZILLA FILM TO END ALL GODZILLA FILMS.

Here, they would bring back *all* of the monsters from the previous movies, and pitch them against each other in one final epic monster brawl. If this were to be the last Godzilla movie, it would be suitably monstrous.

The story is set in the "far future" of 1999, when mankind has established a permanent colony on the moon. Humanity has also found a safe haven for all of Earth's giant monsters: Monsterland. There, beasts such as Godzilla, Mothra, Rodan, Minilla, Anguirus and even monsters from other Toho franchises like Manda, Gorosaurus, and Varan live there among the others, in peace and harmony.

But suddenly, chaos reigns when the monsters inexplicably break free from their manmade bonds and begin attacking cities around the world!

It is revealed that an alien race, the Kilaaks, who also have a secret base on the moon, have taken control of all of Earth's monsters and demand our surrender. A brave team of astronauts infiltrate their moon base and, in a heroic action sequence, they take back control of Earth's mightiest monsters. They are also able to uncover the Kilaaks' mind control techniques, which are currently being used to influence human spies on Earth.

Eventually, the Earthling defense force – now in control of all of the monsters – sends every kaiju to Mount Fuji in an attempt to have them locate and destroy the Kilaaks' earthbound secret base. But the Kilaaks have another trick up their sleeve: the menace from space, King Ghidorah! The monsters are able to team up against the powerful King Ghidorah in a desperate bid to protect planet Earth from total destruction, and the Kilaaks prove they have yet more hidden weapons that they are capable of unleashing.

Eventually, humanity wins the day, and all of the monsters return home, safe and happy on Monsterland.

This is considered one of the best films of the Showa Era. A tour-de-force of special effects wizardry including not only actors in suits, but a thrilling combination of puppetry, pyrotechnics, wirework, and seamless matte paintings that culminate in an historic cinematic mash-up that is both emotionally invested and classic drive-in movie fun.

The human story is equally as engaging, with captivating gunfights, a heroic lead performance by Akira Kubo, and lots of juicy double-crossing by the villainous Kilaaks.

Moments like Mothra and Kumonga teaming up in covering King Ghidorah in their silk spray, or Godzilla attempting to help Rodan when the flying monster is besieged by the deadly and mysterious Fire Dragon, all fill us with excitement as these monsters that have thrilled us and battled one another are now finally joining together in combat against a common foe.

Minilla actually finding a use for his circular ring of Heat Ray in a crucial moment? Perfect. Godzilla discovering the entrance to the Kilaaks' base? Sublime. That final sequence showing all of the monsters on Monsterland essentially waving at us as if to say goodbye, wondering if this would be the final time we would see these monsters on a screen together at all? Both heart-warming and tragic.

But of course, this would be far from the final moment for all of these monsters. *Destroy All Monsters*, without a doubt, proved that Godzilla was here to stay. But for how long? And in what form? And would the original team reunite again for any of its future adventures? Ishiro Honda would indeed return for his next to last time as director of a Godzilla film, and although this next movie is often considered a lesser entry in the canon, Honda would in fact view it as one of his personal favorites...

謎のキラアク星人出現！宇宙をゆるがす11大怪獣の大激闘！

東宝

ムーンライトSY-3号

〈カラー作品〉

怪獣総進撃

ラドン
キングギドラ
バラン
ゴジラ
マンダ
ゴロザウルス
ミニラ
アンギラス
バラゴン
クモンガ
モスラ

監督・本多猪四郎
特技監督・有川貞昌
特技監修・円谷英二
製作・田中友幸
脚本・馬淵薫・本多猪四郎

久保明
小林夕岐子（新人）
愛京子
佐原健二
土屋嘉男
伊藤久哉
黒部進
アンドリュー・ヒューズ
桐野洋雄
田島義文
田崎潤

ゴジラ
モスラ
ラドン
ミニラ
キングギドラ
アンギラス
バラゴン
クモンガ
バラン
マンダ
ゴロザウルス

Opposite: Anguirus' triumphant return to the franchise.

Above: Promotional art of UFO mayhem.

Left: Earth's forces in the Kilaaks' base.

Top (left): Larval Mothra spraying vengeance.

Top (right): Godzilla joins the fray.

Above: Gorosaurus destroys the Arc de Triomphe in Paris.

Opposite: Minilla dances while Anguirus takes a break on set.

Left: The film's monstrous cast assemble for this promotional image

Top: Larval Mothra.

Above (middle): Rodan destroying Russia.

Above: Rodan lands, ready for battle.

Opposite (above): Anguirus roars!.

Opposite (below): Director Ishiro Honda talking to actor Yu Sekita (Anguirus) about a scene.

Right: Minilla.

Below: Behind the scenes photo with Anguirus' discarded shell in the background.

Left: Godzilla wreaking havoc in New York City.

ゴジラ・ミニラ・ガバラ オール怪獣大進撃

ALL MONSTERS ATTACK (1969)

DIRECTOR : ISHIRO HONDA
WRITTEN BY : SHIN'ICHI SEKIZAWA
PRODUCED BY : TOMOYUKI TANAKA
SPECIAL EFFECTS DIRECTOR : AKIRA WATANABE
SCORE : KUNIO MIYAUCHI
STARRING : TOMONORI YAZAKI, HIDEYO AMAMOTO, SACHIO SAKAI, KAZUO SUZUKI, HARUO NAKAJIMA

THE SUCCESS OF *DESTROY ALL MONSTERS* CALLED FOR ANOTHER SEQUEL TO BE QUICKLY PUT IN THE WORKS, AS WAS THE CASE WITH MANY OF THESE TITLES.

A lack of budget meant that the creative team had many hurdles to jump through in order to bring the film to life in the short time frame. Director Honda returned once more to helm the ship, this time with the most restrictions he had yet faced, and the result is an oft-maligned but intimate outlier in the Godzilla franchise. *All Monsters Attack* is a film that showcases Honda's fondness for telling personal human stories, using the monsters as allegory to shine a light on our more human struggles. Only this time, instead of the kaiju standing in for the threat of atomic annihilation, or as biting satire of the television industry, they function as stand-ins for our own personal fears, inadequacies, and ultimate bravery.

The story tells of Ichiro, a young boy who is obsessed with Godzilla and all the other residents of Monster Island. He loves giant monsters, and his very creative imagination leads him frequently to dream of traveling to Monster Island, where he is friends with Minilla. The pair have imaginary adventures on the island, the two frequently helping one another overcome obstacles, or keep up the courage to try harder and stand up for themselves.

Meanwhile, in the real world, Ichiro is bullied by a group of fellow schoolchildren, specifically a child by the name of Sanko Gabara. Whenever Ichiro travels in his mind to Monster Island, he finds that Minilla is also tormented by a monster, a kaiju whose name is *also* Gabara! Together, they devise how to fight it, through bravery and by using their wits.

Ichiro is also unexpectedly caught up in the middle of a heist! Two robbers have stolen a bag of money and are on the run, and Ichiro finds one of their driver's licenses and takes it home – like many young kids, he likes collecting odd treasures that he finds in the world.

The robbers kidnap him, and using the lessons he's learned from Minilla, he must outwit the robbers in order to save himself. He even finds the courage to stand up to his own Gabara, earning the bullies' respect in the process.

Due to the time and budget constraints, one major hurdle this movie has faced critically is that it uses mostly recycled footage from previous Godzilla films for the kaiju battles. Scenes from *Ebirah, Horror of the Deep*, *Son of Godzilla*, and even *King Kong Escapes* are all used, often in their entirety, since there wasn't enough money to film new scenes altogether.

Additionally, this was the first film in which Honda directed not only the human scenes but all of the special effects themselves. *All Monsters Attack* was truly a labor of love for Honda, a small film that focused less on the big monster fights and more on one young child learning how to stand up for himself. While Honda loved the spectacle and undeniable artistry of orchestrating giant monsters rampaging through cities, he also loved the emotional core of the people at the heart of these stories. Here, he was mostly left to do as he pleased within the constraints, and thus we get what feels today almost like a small indie film rather than a kaiju blockbuster.

It's no wonder that he later stated that he considered it one of his favorites of the whole franchise.

Despite the production struggles of *All Monsters Attack*, another sequel was quickly in the works. This one would come from a first-time director, and would prove to be one of the most unique entries of the entire franchise...

"ALL MONSTERS ATTACK IS A FILM THAT SHOWCASES HONDA'S FONDNESS FOR TELLING PERSONAL HUMAN STORIES, USING THE MONSTERS AS ALLEGORY TO SHINE A LIGHT ON OUR MORE HUMAN STRUGGLES."

東宝
ずらりならんだ九人怪獣世紀の決戦！
ゴジラ親子の大ピンチ
怪獣島の王座を狙う
猛烈新怪獣ガバラ登場！
ゴジラ・ミニラ・ガバラ
〈カラー作品〉
オール怪獣大進撃
ゴジラ
ミニラ
ガバラ
カマキラス
ゴロザウルス
エビラ
クモンガ
映倫

Top: Promotional artwork of Ichiro fleeing the many monsters he faces in his dream world.

Right: Promotional art of the epic monster battle.

Opposite: Behind the scenes photo of Gabara on set, with stage lights and scaffolding visible above.

Opposite (above): Promotional material for *All Monsters Attack*.

Opposite (below): Gabara facing down his miniscule foes.

Right: Minilla to the rescue.

Below: Godzilla steps in to save the day against Gabara.

ゴジラ対ヘドラ

GODZILLA VS. HEDORAH (1971)

DIRECTOR : YOSHIMITSU BANNO
WRITTEN BY : YOSHIMITSU BANNO, TAKESHI KIMURA, TOMOYUKI TANAKA
SPECIAL EFFECTS DIRECTOR : TERUYOSHI NAKANO
SCORE : RIICHIRO MANABE
STARRING : AKIRA YAMAUCHI, TOSHIE KIMURA, HIROYUKI KAWASE, KENPACHIRO SATSUMA, HARUO NAKAJIMA

NEWCOMER YOSHIMITSU BANNO, A TV DIRECTOR AND FORMER ASSISTANT DIRECTOR FOR AKIRA KUROSAWA, WAS BROUGHT IN TO HELM GODZILLA'S NEW ADVENTURE FACING OFF AGAINST AN ORIGINAL FOE: HEDORAH, AKA THE SMOG MONSTER.

The film is a psychedelic indictment of mankind's pollution of the earth, with Godzilla no longer a proxy for the destructive nature of man, but instead of the earth itself. Godzilla here is protector, a natural response to the man-created Hedorah, a being originally from space that becomes mutated by the toxic sludge filling our oceans and skies.

The story follows a scientist and his family after they discover what appears to be a living tadpole made out of inorganic material. It is a being that shouldn't be alive... but is. And it is made of pure pollution. What's more, anything it touches corrodes, and the more contaminated matter it devours, the larger and more dangerous it becomes.

Godzilla challenges Hedorah multiple times, but every time Hedorah only grows more powerful. Even if Godzilla forces him to retreat, the bits of pollution that are expelled simply crawl back to merge with it, allowing it to evolve and grow!

Eventually, thousands perish as a result of Hedorah's attacks, and a group of young people holds a kind of vigil for humanity at the base of Mount Fuji. One final night of music and fun before the world ends the next day (made even more bleak by the use of black and white photography during part of this sequence). But Godzilla arrives to challenge Hedorah again... and loses! Hedorah overpowers our monstrous hero, even going so far as to injure one of Godzilla's eyes.

All hope seems lost before the army builds a final hope for a last stand: a huge electricity array that will hopefully dry out the beast. And Godzilla arrives to help, prompting the final epic – and exceedingly slimy – final battle.

This film is a divisive entry to Godzilla fans, not least because it is stylistically one of the boldest films in the franchise. Psychedelic dance sequences, animated sections, musical numbers, even Godzilla suddenly having the ability to fly... they all come together in an unforgettable movie that is pulp entertainment but with a very clear environmental message.

The design of the Hedorah suit is also one of the more unique in the franchise. Built by former Godzilla special effects assistant Teruyoshi Nakano, it features a number of unique forms, as it evolves from fight to fight. In addition to its original amphibious form, it sprouts wings and flies, and of course stands upright, blinking out with its striking red and green eyes. The special effects in this film are particularly visceral, with Godzilla jamming its hands into Hedorah's eye sockets, black sludge spurting like blood, or huge tentacles of black sludge oozing down the stairs of a nightclub like a scene out of *The Blob*. You truly believe that this is a creature made purely from the filth mankind has carelessly dumped away.

Left: Promotional material for Godzilla vs. Hedorah

流れ星でやって来た
公害怪獣ヘドラ！
街を森をふみつぶし
二大怪獣が大決戦！

ゴジラ対ヘドラ

《カラー作品》

One particularly interesting bit of trivia from behind the scenes of this movie is that the actor who played Hedorah suffered appendicitis while filming, and due to the length of time it would have taken to remove his suit, they had to perform the surgery on set *while he was still dressed as Hedorah!* That's kaiju commitment.

Veteran *Godzilla* producer Tomoyuki Tanaka famously disliked this film, and brought in Honda to give notes in order to help the final product. Despite the master's help, Tanaka still felt the wild eco-friendly allegory strayed too far from Godzilla's path, and Banno's future would be summed up by the text at the end of the film which reads, "Will there be another one?". There was a clear answer: no.

Banno did indeed have a sequel planned involving Hedorah returning and wreaking havoc once again, but due to Tanaka's disappointment in the film's final product, that sequel wouldn't happen. Banno would go on to work on more Godzilla sequels, however, as a producer on Gareth Edwards' *Godzilla* in 2014, and posthumously as executive producer on *Godzilla: King of the Monsters* and *Godzilla vs. Kong*.

Toho would return to form with Godzilla's next outing the following year, bringing back a familiar director as well as a number of classic monsters. It would also mark the final time Haruo Nakajima would play the icon he had portrayed in every film since Honda's original...

Opposite: Kenpachiro Satsuma as Hedorah.

Above: Godzilla under attack by Hedorah's flying form.

Top (left): Godzilla's iconic backwards flight.

Top (right): Citizens fleeing a marauding Hedorah.

Above: Hedorah emerging from the toxic ocean.

Opposite: Behind-the-scenes picture of Godzilla in mid-air.

Left: Hedorah versus a street of intricate miniatures.

Top: Hedorah hurtling through the air.

Above (middle): Hedorah's flying form.

Above: Behind the scenes photo of Hedorah emerging from the pool on set.

Top: Promotional artwork of Godzilla battling Hedorah.

Left: Godzilla with a flying kick to Hedorah's face.

Above: Behind the scenes photo, with stage lights visible above the backdrop.

Opposite: Hedorah takes a smoke break.

地球攻撃命令　ゴジラ対ガイガン

GODZILLA VS. GIGAN (1972)

DIRECTOR : JUN FUKUDA
WRITTEN BY : SHIN'ICHI SEKIZAWA
PRODUCED BY : TOMOYUKI TANAKA
SPECIAL EFFECTS DIRECTOR : TERUYOSHI NAKANO
SCORE : AKIRA IFUKUBE
STARRING : HIROSHI ISHIKAWA, YURIKO HISHIMI, MINORU TAKASHIMA, TOMOKO UMEDA, HARUO NAKAJIMA

AFTER THE DIFFERENT DIRECTION OF *GODZILLA VS. HEDORAH*, GODZILLA RETURNS IN A FILM THAT HARKENS BACK TO THE PREVIOUS HONDA-DIRECTED GIANT MONSTER BRAWLS.

In *Godzilla vs. Gigan*, a race of shape-shifting cockroach aliens have been driven from their home due to the human-like species there rendering it inhabitable due to pollution. These aliens have chosen Earth as their new home, and, assuming fake human forms, plot to take over the world using two monsters from space. One of them is very familiar to Godzilla fans: King Ghidorah! Godzilla's longtime nemesis returns alongside a new foe, the robotic, bird-like, razor-clawed Gigan.

The aliens' cover is a Godzilla-themed amusement park that claims to promote world peace, the centerpiece of which is a 160-foot tall Godzilla Tower, where children will be able to ride to the top for a thrilling view.

A manga artist who is hired to draw concept art for this park soon learns that their plan to "promote peace" is, once the park is complete, to destroy Monster Island – and Godzilla and all of the other monsters with it! They claim this will finally achieve true peace for the planet.

The manga artist (Gengo) inadvertently finds one of the tapes that will be used to summon Gigan and King Ghidorah to Earth, and upon playing it alerts Godzilla and its onetime foe (now turned ally) Anguirus on Monster Island. They have a conversation – one of the great Showa Era Godzilla scenes, where comic-book-style speech bubbles are used to tell us what Godzilla and Anguirus are saying to each other – and Anguirus is sent to Japan to investigate.

Eventually, as the artist and his friends unravel the aliens' plot (and narrowly avoid disaster thanks to Gengo's wife's martial arts skills), Gigan and King Ghidorah arrive on Earth and begin wreaking havoc. Godzilla joins Anguirus to fight them to save the planet, and one of the longest continuous battles in the Era ensues, with Gigan, King Ghidorah, Anguirus, and Godzilla in a two-on-two brawl on the site of the new theme park.

The humans' plot to overthrow the aliens continues while the monsters fight, and eventually we see peace restored and Godzilla swimming back to live in peace on Monster Island.

This would be the final film in which Haruo Nakajima – the original Godzilla actor – would play the famous kaiju. The final moments, where Godzilla even turns around towards us to give one final roar, are touching and befitting of the end of his legendary twelve-film run as the King of the Monsters.

Godzilla vs. Gigan has themes of the overreach of technology (the aliens constantly tout the supremacy of their technology, versus Gengo's mistrust of computers and insistence that human ingenuity and persistence will always win the day). And despite its tonal difference from *Godzilla vs. Hedorah*, the anti-pollution themes of that film carry over into this, with the astonishing allegory of a race of cockroaches that had to leave their planet because their humans destroyed it so much as to make it uninhabitable even for them!

Fukuda would return to direct the next instalment in the franchise the following year, one that would prove to be a fan favorite, introducing one of Godzilla's most enduring and iconic allies...

Below: A behind the scenes shot shows King Ghidorah looming.

東宝
地球攻撃命令
ゴジラ対ガイガン
ゴジラ・ガイガン・アンギラス・キングギドラ/石川博・菱見百合子・梅田智子/西沢利明・高島稔・藤田漸・村井国夫・清水元
映倫

Opposite: Godzilla Tower miniature on set; notice the visible folds in the studio fabric behind.

Above: Anguirus ready for action.

Below: Behind the scenes photo of King Ghidorah suspended from the ceiling of Toho Studios.

Right: King Ghidorah, wings unfurled.

Left: Promotional material for Godzilla vs. Gigan.

Top: The foes meet in battle.

Above (middle): King Ghidorah in mid-attack.

Above: The final showdown.

Opposite: Promotional image showing Gigan's deadly eye laser, a weapon that never was shown in the film.

Above: Anguirus on set, resting its legs before the next scene.

Top (left): Godzilla's Heat Ray in promotional materials.

Top (right): Gigan in black and white.

Left: Godzilla and Gigan locked in battle.

Above: Gigan, full color.

Above: Gigan showing off its battle pose.

ゴジラ対メガロ

GODZILLA VS. MEGALON (1973)

DIRECTOR : JUN FUKUDA
WRITTEN BY : JUN FUKUDA
PRODUCED BY : TOMOYUKI TANAKA
SPECIAL EFFECTS DIRECTOR : TERUYOSHI NAKANO
SCORE : RIICHIRO MANABE
STARRING : KATSUHIKO SASAKI, HIROYUKI KAWASE, YUTAKA HAYASHI, TSUGUTOSHI KOMADA, SHINJI TAKAGI

IN 1972, TOHO HELD A CONTEST FOR SCHOOLCHILDREN, TASKING THEM WITH DESIGNING A NEW MONSTER THAT WOULD APPEAR IN THE NEXT GODZILLA FILM.

A young boy won the top prize for his design of a creature he called Red Alone, which would evolve into the fan favorite, fighting robot Jet Jaguar!

In *Godzilla vs. Megalon* a kingdom of undersea dwellers called the Seatopians are angered when the humans above harm their aquatic utopia with more nuclear bomb tests. Vowing to get revenge on the humans that have been destroying their home, they call upon the giant beetle god that they worship – known as Megalon – to rise to the surface and destroy the world!

But, where to send Megalon? It doesn't know what cities to destroy, so the Seatopians decide that he needs a guide. So, they send a team of Seatopian spies to the surface to steal a newly-built robot, Jet Jaguar, and use his ability of flight (with some reprogramming, of course) to guide Megalon around the earth on a tour of destruction.

Fortunately, the inventors of Jet Jaguar are able to quickly re-establish communication with the robot (who we have learned can grow to enormous size!) and send him on a quest to Monster Island to fetch Godzilla and guide it back to Japan, where it will fight Megalon and save the world once more. Similarly, the Seatopians call upon their extraterrestrial friends (the Space Hunter Nebula M, aliens from *Godzilla vs. Gigan*) to send Gigan back to Earth to fight on the side of Megalon.

What results is a monster melee featuring exceptional wirework and a highly detailed design for Megalon – which at this point was the heaviest suit Toho had ever built after the original Godzilla suit in 1954!

Jun Fukuda returns and brings his signature brand of child-friendly kaiju action, including several moments that have come to be symbols of the entire franchise: Godzilla's sliding kick into Megalon, and the iconic handshake of friendship between Godzilla and Jet Jaguar at the end of the battle. A pop song all about Jet Jaguar also closes out the film, cementing this as one of Godzilla's most memorable and childlike outings.

Due to delays in the schedule, this was also one of the most quickly-made films of the entire franchise, going from inception of the idea to world premiere in six months! The entire movie was shot in three weeks, and the pace was so fast that they didn't even have time to write a full script. They simply had an outline and made up dialogue on the spot.

This shoot may have been wildly paced and fraught with challenges, but the end result remains a fan favorite, with Jet Jaguar quickly cemented as one of the Godzilla franchise's most enduring and lovable heroes. And although he wouldn't appear in another Godzilla film, he is a major character in the television series *Godzilla Island*, as well as the popular comic series *Godzilla: Rulers of Earth*.

Jet Jaguar's legacy as a friend of Godzilla is undeniable, but as the Showa Era began to draw to a close, Toho would introduce a new menace that countered Jet Jaguar's positive technology with a robotic foe that was altogether deadly and sinister...

"WHAT RESULTS IS A MONSTER MELEE FEATURING EXCEPTIONAL WIREWORK AND A HIGHLY DETAILED DESIGN FOR MEGALON – WHICH AT THIS POINT WAS THE HEAVIEST SUIT TOHO HAD EVER BUILT."

海底王国のすごいやつメガロ！傷だらけのゴジラ必殺のウルトラC！
東宝
《カラー作品》
ゴジラ対メガロ
佐々木勝彦
川瀬裕之
林ゆたか
原作■関沢新
メガロ
ジェット・ジャガー
ガイガン
ゴジラ
映倫
Printed in Japan © TOHO CO., Ltd.

Above: The full gang posing for promotional materials.

Below: Godzilla about to unleash arboreal vengeance.

Right: Jet Jaguar, seen here in a promotional image.

Opposite: Jet Jaguar, the newest member of the Kaiju team.

Left: Megalon destroying a bridge in a pivotal scene from the film.

Top: Jet Jaguar in front of Mount Fuji.

Above: The epic final melee.

Left: Megalon and Gigan teaming up.

Below: Godzilla strikes a samurai-like pose to protect Jet Jaguar.

Opposite: Promotional photo of Megalon and its destructive abilities.

ゴジラ対メカゴジラ

GODZILLA VS. MECHAGODZILLA (1974)

DIRECTOR : JUN FUKUDA
WRITTEN BY : JUN FUKUDA
PRODUCED BY : TOMOYUKI TANAKA
SPECIAL EFFECTS DIRECTOR : TERUYOSHI NAKANO
SCORE : MASARU SATO
STARRING : MASAAKI DAIMON, KAZUYA AOYAMA, REIKO TAJIMA, AKIHIKO HIRATA, ISAO ZUSHI

FOR GODZILLA'S 20TH ANNIVERSARY, DIRECTOR JUN FUKUDA RETURNED FOR ONE FINAL ADVENTURE WITH THE KAIJU.

This time, he would pit Godzilla against a new foe: the alien-controlled Mechagodzilla, with help from its old friend Anguirus and a new ally: the mystical, slumbering King Caesar.

In the story, an Azumi priestess (Azumi being one of Japan's most ancient religions) has a premonition of horrible destruction. At the same time, a group of archaeologists discover, deep in a mountain in Okinawa in the south of Japan, a mysterious metal that appears to be from space. In addition, they find ancient markings that tell of a prophecy, that when a black mountain appears above the clouds, a monster will arrive to destroy humanity. But, when the "sun rises in the west", King Caesar will appear with another monster, and they will fight the villain and save mankind.

Sure enough, a black cloud that looks just like Mount Fuji appears in the sky and Godzilla emerges from the mountain!

Shockingly, the friendly Godzilla is on a path to utter destruction. Its friend Anguirus appears and attempts to stop Godzilla, but Godzilla chooses to fight instead. Not only does he battle the monster, but it nearly kills Anguirus! In one of the most violent moments of the series thus far, Godzilla mortally wounds its longtime kaiju ally, and is left to destroy as it likes. Godzilla begins wreaking havoc just like its old self, with no apparent way to stop its rampage.

Just then, however, a *second Godzilla* appears and battles what we will learn is an imposter. This is not some suddenly evil Godzilla. This is Mechagodzilla!

A huge robot version of Godzilla that can fly and shoot powerful beams from its eyes has appeared on Earth, and we learn it is being controlled by a race of shape-shifting aliens (whose natural form is that of apemen, who look strikingly similar to the popular *Planet of the Apes* characters that were also gracing cinema screens at the time).

These aliens – who inhabit the "Third Planet of the Black Hole" – hope to conquer Earth using this super weapon. While these aliens attempt to steal the hieroglyph-adorned statue of King Caesar so that they may control the ancient monster, the archaeologists plot a daring heist to break into the aliens' underground base and dismantle Mechagodzilla from the inside.

All of this culminates, of course, in a massive battle between Godzilla, Mechagodzilla, and a newly awoken King Caesar. The Black Hole Aliens are foiled, and King Caesar proves himself as another ally to mankind just like Godzilla.

Godzilla vs. Mechagodzilla is one of the most colorful of the entire franchise, with bright Technicolor animation bringing Mechagodzilla's powerful eye beams to life, and the bright-green blood of the Black Hole Aliens a stark contrast against the sleek metallic sheen of their futuristic alien base.

Speaking of blood, this film is also one of the most violent in the franchise. After special effects master Eiji Tsuburaya passed away a few years previously, the new special effects teams began to pull the series away from his family-friendly ideal and into more adult territory. Bright-red blood flows from the kaiju as they battle, aliens get shot in the neck, jungle-green blood spraying like something out of a Tarantino film. Even Mechagodzilla's destruction is particularly violent.

All of these elements combined with some cutting-edge animation work and one of the more complex human stories have made *Godzilla vs. Mechagodzilla* one of the most beloved films in the entire franchise. Jun Fukuda brought a fast-paced television sensibility to his run of Godzilla films, and the tone he set would be one that defined Godzilla for a generation. With *Godzilla vs. Mechagodzilla* he ended his tenure with the kaiju on a high note, introducing two new monsters that would be beloved characters for the rest of the franchise, as well as giving poor Anguirus its final (and very memorable) appearance in a Godzilla film for the next 30 years.

But Toho couldn't close out the Showa Era without one final epic adventure, a direct sequel to this film that would bring back Godzilla's original creator, Ishiro Honda, one final time...

宇宙をとび ミサイルを撃ち込む！全身が武器の凄いゴジラが現われた！

東宝チャンピオンまつり

ゴジラ誕生20周年記念映画

キングシーサー

ゴジラ

メカゴジラ

アンギラス

ゴジラ対メカゴジラ

（カラー作品）

大門正明
青山一也
田島令子
ベルベラ・リーン
松下ひろみ
平田昭彦
睦五郎
岸田森
小泉博

監督●福田純
特撮監督●中野昭慶
製作●田中友幸

東宝

Opposite (above): King Caesar, Mechagodzilla, and Godzilla meet up for a final showdown.

Opposite (below): King Caesar and Mechagodzilla face off, one an ancient mystical being, the other a futuristic alien.

Top: King Caesar, appearing for the first time in this film.

Left: Mechagodzilla being prepped for takeoff.

Above: A black and white draft of what would ultimately become the key art for the film.

メカゴジラの逆襲

TERROR OF MECHAGODZILLA (1975)

DIRECTOR : ISHIRO HONDA
WRITTEN BY : YUKIKO TAKAYAMA
PRODUCED BY : TOMOYUKI TANAKA
SPECIAL EFFECTS DIRECTOR : TERUYOSHI NAKANO
SCORE : AKIRA IFUKUBE
STARRING : KATSUHIRO SASAKI, TOMOKO AI, AKIHIKO HIRATA, KATSUMASA UCHIDA, TORU KAWAI

ISHIRO HONDA RETURNS ONE LAST TIME TO THE FRANCHISE AND MONSTER THAT HE BIRTHED, WORKING FROM A SCRIPT THAT WON A STORY CONTEST TOHO HAD HELD THE YEAR BEFORE.

The screenplay would be reworked to include Godzilla's newest – and very popular – nemesis, Mechagodzilla, and would also break form in being a direct sequel to the previous film, picking up only days after *Godzilla vs. Mechagodzilla*'s end.

Honda would also return to his more serious horror roots, crafting one of the franchise's darkest entries to date. Not only violent, it is also centered around complex themes of parental abuse and vengeful cruelty.

The story begins with a group of Interpol agents searching the ocean floor, looking for Mechagodzilla's remains in an effort to better understand the aliens who created it (here called Simeons, a more succinct and elegant name than Black Hole Aliens, which they'd been before).

The submarine stumbles upon a new creature called Titanosaurus, which destroys the boat and leaves the topside scientists stumped. They enlist the aid of a marine biologist who is able to link the Titanosaurus to a reclusive scientist by the name of Shinzo Mafune, who had great interest in the monster because Mafune wished to destroy the world!

They visit Dr. Mafune's house and encounter his daughter, who lies to the agents, insisting that her father is dead and that she had destroyed all of his notes. Of course, this is not true, and soon we learn that not only has Dr. Mafune developed technology that would allow him to control Titanosaurus (thus expediting his desire to see the world burn), but he is also teaming up with the Simeons to rebuild Mechagodzilla! With Mechagodzilla and Titanosaurus teamed up together, they'd be unstoppable!

Throughout all of this, Dr. Mafune's daughter falls in love with the marine biologist, and we learn that she is in fact a cyborg! It appears her father had pieced her back together in a bid to save her from succumbing to his devious experiments upon her when she was a child. There are many layers to this striking film.

Of course, when Titanosaurus and Mechagodzilla are unleashed upon Tokyo, Godzilla appears to battle the two titans and save Japan once again. Sadly, many of our human characters are lost throughout this drama, with one in particular making a tragic self-sacrifice and dying in their lover's arms.

Honda always wanted to direct Godzilla films with an eye for human emotion and with a flair for the serious and frightening, and here he truly fires on all cylinders. Bringing back iconic series composer Akira Ifukube, Honda instills a real sense of dread and danger into every frame of *Terror of Mechagodzilla*.

Boundaries were also pushed, and not only in terms of the violence and adult themes. This film is one of only two Godzilla films to feature nudity, during a brief sequence when Dr. Mafune's cyborg daughter Katsura is being operated upon. The special effects also reach an all-time high here, between the new Mechagodzilla 2 suit to the intricate clockwork parts inside of Katsura's human skin, it's clear that Honda and Teruyoshi Nakano (the special effects director) were leaving nothing on the table.

Despite glowing reviews from critics praising Honda's return to the franchise, *Terror of Mechagodzilla* performed poorly at the box office, largely due to a general decline in interest in monster movies at the time. Toho made the tough decision to put a pause on the Godzilla franchise, and so Honda's final shot of Godzilla wading away into the sunset would prove to be not only his final moment working on his beloved film series, but also the end of the Showa Era as a whole. Honda's love for his creation was evident from the first frame until the last, and *Terror of Mechagodzilla* serves as a fitting farewell to the true father of Godzilla.

Godzilla would lie dormant for nearly a decade, sleeping, ready to emerge when called once more. When it awoke again, however, it was no longer the friendly savior that it had become. On the 30th anniversary of the first iconic film, Godzilla would return in its original, terrifying role, and in a new, very different era for the King of the Monsters...

東宝チャンピオンまつり

さらに狂暴となって！さらに　な武器を持って！メカゴジラがよみがえった！
地球を奪え！――宇宙人の　に新怪獣・チタノザウルスと日本中を大破壊！

メカゴジラ2

チタノザウルス

ゴジラ

最新作メカゴジラ・シリーズ第2弾

メカゴジラの逆襲

東宝

映倫 74536

製作・東宝映像株式会社
配給・東宝株式会社

光学撮影・真野田嘉一
合成・三瓶一信
特殊効果・渡辺忠昭
操演・松本光司
特撮スタッフ
音楽・伊福部昭
照明・高島利雄
録音・矢野口文雄
美術・本多好文
撮影・富岡素敬
脚本・高山由紀子
製作・田中友幸
特撮監督・中野昭慶
監督・本多猪四郎

《カラー作品》

佐々木勝彦
藍とも子（新人）
大門正明
内田勝正
麻里とも恵
六本木真
伊吹徹
中丸忠雄
睦五郎
平田昭彦

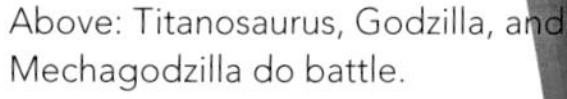

Above: Titanosaurus, Godzilla, and Mechagodzilla do battle.

Above (left): Promotional art of the three kaiju together.

Right: Titanosaurus wreaking havoc

Right: Mechagodzilla, terrifying.

VSシリーズ

THE HEISEI ERA

The Heisei Era of the Godzilla franchise began with *The Return of Godzilla* in 1984, all the way until *Godzilla vs. Destoroyah* in 1995. This period of Godzilla's reign is most notable for being the most adult-oriented of the eras, with themes of death, loss, and tragedy running through all of the films. Cold War-era nuclear fears seep through the pores of the franchise during this time period, as do a general mistrust of technology, and humanity's hubris in sticking our fingers where they don't belong.

Of course, that means Godzilla must arrive to set us on the right path. That's not to say there's no fun to be had here. Time travel, ancient magic, and the adorable return of a Godzilla-like infant make the Heisei Era a layered and complex period for Godzilla and its friends and foes, and the fact that a single cohesive arc joins all of the films in one continuity also makes this era particularly enjoyable to follow as a Godzilla fan. So dive in as Godzilla returns, no longer a savior to humanity, but a villain once again...

THE HEISEI ERA FILMS ARE:

THE RETURN OF GODZILLA (1984) • GODZILLA VS. BIOLLANTE (1989) • GODZILLA VS. KING GHIDORAH (1991) • GODZILLA VS. MOTHRA (1992) GODZILLA VS. MECHAGODZILLA II (1993) • GODZILLA VS. SPACEGODZILLA (1994) GODZILLA VS. DESTOROYAH (1995)

ゴジラ

THE RETURN OF GODZILLA (1984)

DIRECTOR : KOJI HASHIMOTO
WRITTEN BY : HIDEICHI NAGAHARA
PRODUCED BY : NORIO HAYASHI, KIYOMI KANAZAWA
SPECIAL EFFECTS DIRECTOR : TERUYOSHI NAKANO
SCORE : REIJIRO KOROKU
STARRING : KEIJU KOBAYASHI, KEN TANAKA, YASUKO SAWAGUCHI, SHIN TAKUMA, YOSUKE NATSUKI

AFTER NEARLY 10 YEARS IN CINEMATIC HIBERNATION, PRODUCER TOMOYUKI TANAKA WOULD REVIVE GODZILLA IN DRAMATIC AND DARK FASHION WITH 1984'S *THE RETURN OF GODZILLA*, AND HE WOULD DO SO BY BRINGING GODZILLA BACK TO ITS HORROR ROOTS.

Gone was the family-friendly fun that defined most of the Showa Era, replaced here with an angry Godzilla bent once more on destruction, a new representation of nuclear fears in the midst of the Cold War.

The film does away with all of the continuity from the previous films except for the original, its opening itself an echo of how the entire franchise began. A fishing vessel finds itself in trouble when a nearby volcano begins to erupt, and a gargantuan monster emerges from the flames. Godzilla, it appears, has returned.

There is only one survivor of the incident, shaken and desperate to share news of Godzilla's emergence with the world, but the government stifles a reporter's interview in order to keep the presence of Godzilla a secret. Meanwhile, a Soviet nuclear submarine is destroyed somewhere in the Pacific, and of course the Soviets are convinced that the Americans must be to blame. Global tensions were already at an all-time high, and now the Soviets and Americans have their fingers on the triggers of all-out nuclear war.

The Japanese government – memories of Godzilla's attack 30 years prior still fresh in their minds – worry that he will head once more for Tokyo. They reveal a secret weapon, a flying tank called the Super X that they hope will be powerful enough to protect Tokyo from the rampaging monster.

Soon enough, all efforts to keep Godzilla's return a secret are proven moot, as it begins to attack nuclear power plants, growing in strength as it does so.

This of course becomes a matter of global concern, with the Americans and the Soviets clamoring to attack Godzilla with nuclear weapons. The Japanese of course notice the lack of concern over foreign powers wanting to detonate yet another nuclear weapon on Japanese soil, and flatly refuse. There is a moment where one of the aides to the prime minister insists that to the Americans and the Soviets, their concern is not for the safety of the people of Japan, nor for the destruction of Godzilla... but instead simply to be able to have an excuse to test their weaponry in an urban setting. A haunting, poignant, and sobering reminder that Godzilla is a mirror to humanity's greatest failings.

Japan of course forbids the use of nuclear weapons and forms a plan to lure Godzilla away with a high-tech homing beacon, guiding it to a volcano where the monster can be buried, destroyed far away from the millions of residents of Tokyo. The Soviets have their own secret plan, however, and prep a missile to launch from orbit as soon as Godzilla enters the city.

All of these various chess pieces converge in a final act that features daring helicopter rescues, near-miss nuclear disasters, and of course the stunning and devastating destruction of Tokyo. The blast of a nuclear missile in orbit turns the skies a lush, blood red, a fittingly ominous backdrop for Godzilla's frightening, yet elegant path of ruin. Echoing the original film, we spend time with characters that ultimately will tragically perish, bringing gravitas to remind audiences why Godzilla is a creature to be respected and feared.

The original concept for this new iteration of Godzilla was born of the recent spate of popular horror sci-fi films, like *Alien*, *Invasion of the Body Snatchers*, and the 1976 reboot of *King Kong* from Dino De Laurentiis. In addition, the Three Mile Island disaster of 1979 was an appropriate backdrop for bringing cinema's most famous embodiment of nuclear fear back from the dead.

Ishiro Honda was approached to direct once again, but was not only busy working with Akira Kurosawa on a number of films, he reportedly felt that the franchise had run its course. In any case, it was a new era and that meant a time for new blood. Koji Hashimoto, who had been Assistant Director on a number of the Showa Era films, would be tapped to direct this as his first film, and his clear admiration of Honda's work shows through in the final product. *The Return of Godzilla* is bleak and ends on a note of almost nihilistic sadness, a tone that would flow through all of the Heisei Era films.

日本を呑むか、地球を壊すか
80メートル、5万トン
列島をひき裂く巨大怪獣——
もう誰も…
ヤツを止められない!
30年間の沈黙を破って全世界待望の「ゴジラ」最新作!
ゴジラ
GODZILLA
小林桂樹
田中健
沢口靖子
宅麻伸
石坂浩二
武田鉄矢
(特別出演)
夏木陽介
製作・原案■田中友幸/協力製作■田中文雄
脚本■永原秀一/特技監督■中野昭慶
監督■橋本幸治
ドルビーステレオ方式 DOLBY STEREO
東宝

Teruyoshi Nakano returned to direct the special effects, and a new Godzilla suit was built that would be considerably larger in scale than in the previous era. In addition, a fully articulated 16-foot tall animatronic Godzilla was designed for close-up shots, giving the monster more expression than ever before.

It was a dark time for the world in the early 1980s, with global tensions wound tight and the threat of nuclear war extremely tangible. This environment was ripe for Godzilla to re-emerge as a reminder to humanity that with such mighty weaponry at our fingertips also comes tremendous responsibility, and respect for life itself.

It would be five years before Godzilla would return to the big screen, this time back to squaring off against another kaiju foe, perhaps the most unique and unsettling of all of Toho's creations...

Above: Godzilla, with an all-new, angrier scowl.

Right: Godzilla returns more mean than ever.

Opposite: Godzilla at its most imposing yet.

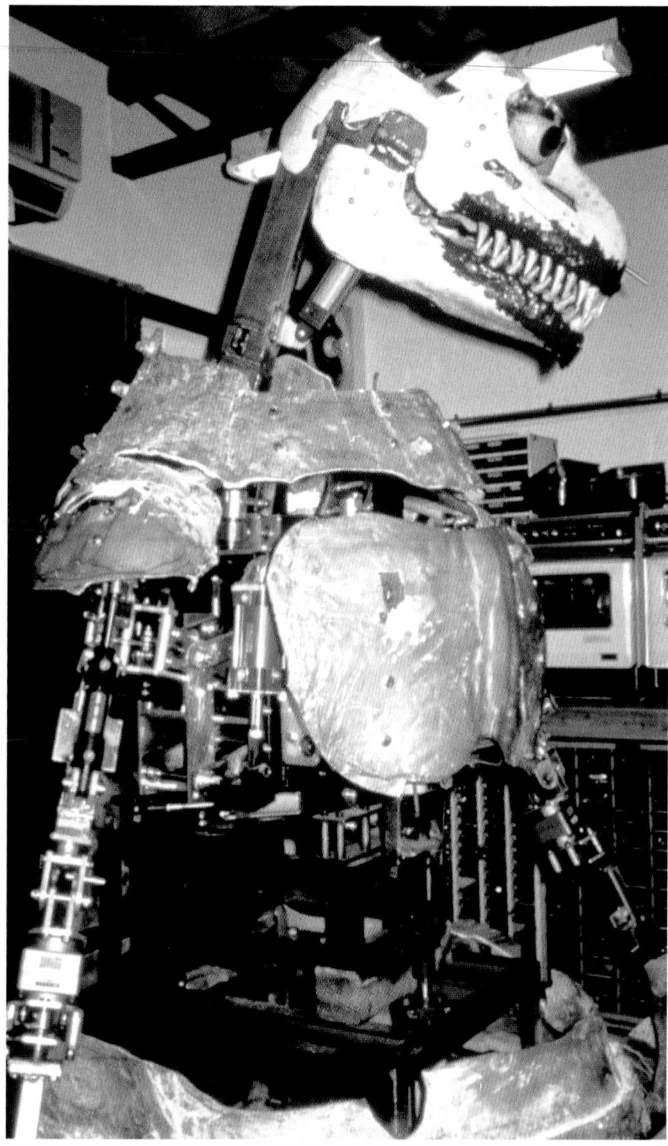

Top: Skinless animatronic Godzilla, used for highly detailed close-ups.

Above: Godzilla finally falls.

Right: Godzilla returns to Tokyo Bay.

ゴジラvsビオランテ

GODZILLA VS BIOLLANTE (1989)

DIRECTOR : KAZUKI OHMORI
WRITTEN BY : KAZUKI OHMORI
PRODUCED BY : SHOGO TOMIYAMA
SPECIAL EFFECTS DIRECTOR : KOICHI KAWAKITA
SCORE : KOICHI SUGIYAMA
STARRING : KUNIHIKO MITAMURA, YOSHIKO TANAKA, MASANOBU TAKASHIMA, KOJI TAKAHASHI, TORU MINEGISHI, MEGUMI ODAKA, KENPACHIRO SATSUMA

BORN FROM A PUBLIC STORY-WRITING CONTEST, *GODZILLA VS. BIOLLANTE* WOULD VEER AWAY FROM THEMES OF NUCLEAR FEARS, AND INSTEAD TACKLE UNCERTAINTY AND DEBATE OVER THE RELATIVELY NEW FIELD OF GENETIC RESEARCH AND BIOTECHNOLOGY.

Picking up immediately after the destruction of Tokyo at the end of *The Return of Godzilla*, scientists gather some of Godzilla's cells in hopes of using them to genetically modify plants that will grow in even the most arid desert. Geneticist Dr. Shiragami and his daughter Erika are working together on the project when a terrorist bombing destroys the lab, tragically killing his daughter.

Five years later, we find Dr. Shiragami merging some of Erika's cells with those of a rose from her favorite rose garden, in an attempt to scientifically preserve part of her soul. Meanwhile, the government is attempting to use Godzilla's cells to develop a weapon that can fight Godzilla should the monster ever emerge from the volcano. Dr. Shiragami refuses their request to work on the project, still in mourning from the loss of his daughter.

Amidst all this, several different factions from around the world are attempting to steal the Godzilla cells, and eventually threaten to free Godzilla from its volcanic prison should the government not hand them over. After a number of double-crosses, Godzilla is indeed released, and disaster appears imminent as it begins making its way toward the nearest power plant.

At this point, Dr. Shiragami agrees to join the project and upon gaining access to the precious Godzilla cells, cannot resist splicing them with his rose/daughter hybrid cells. The result, we soon learn, is that he has created an all-new monster: Biollante.

Biollante begins as a formless mass of plant-based tentacles, but once it escapes into the bay it grows quickly to staggering size, taller than Godzilla, and takes the form of a gargantuan rose. It's a beautiful, ominous sight, the massive rose creature troublingly silent and still.

We are introduced to a character in this film that will go on to be a major recurring character throughout the Heisei Era: psychic Miki Saegusa, who can use her powers to influence Godzilla, and even read its thoughts. She is able to guide Godzilla towards Biollante, who quickly attacks using razor-toothed root tentacles.

Establishing a theme that would also become popular during the Heisei Era (one that began with *Godzilla vs. Hedorah* back in 1971), Biollante goes through several stages of evolution throughout the film. Her first form feels like something out of John Carpenter's *The Thing*, and while her second form is an image of sinister beauty, her third and final form is outright terrifying. A massive beast much larger than Godzilla, with snapping jaws full of razor-sharp teeth and barbs on the end of her tentacles that impale Godzilla straight through its body in gory fashion.

The final battle between the two is a full-on horror movie, the nightmarish Biollante unleashing a torrent of violence on Godzilla, who is barely hanging on for its life. Eventually, Biollante will evolve once more, with an ending that leaves little doubt that Dr. Shiragami did indeed succeed in preserving his daughter's soul.

Left: Biollante's frightening final form.

超ゴジラ
それはゴジラ細胞から生まれた!
'90年正月映画日本代表!
ゴジラ
VS
ビオランテ
製作■田中友幸 脚本・監督■大森一樹 特技監督■川北紘一
★ゴジラストーリー応募作品「ゴジラ対ビオランテ」小林晋一郎・作より
音楽■すぎやま こういち(サントラ盤)東芝EMI/ゴジラテーマ曲■伊福部 昭
三田村邦彦・田中好子/高嶋政伸・小高恵美・峰岸 徹
沢口靖子・永島敏行・久我美子/金田龍之介・高橋幸治

Opposite: Lights, camera, action! A behind the scenes look at Biollante on set.

Top: Biollante's final form, deadly tentacles flailing.

Above: Godzilla and Biollante face off at last.

It's a wild plot, with a detailed spy movie subplot that feels like something out of a James Bond film. There's a sadness to this movie, as well, a deep sense of loss and a rumination on how far is too far, when it comes to scientific research. Yet again, Godzilla is here to remind us that humility must outweigh hubris when playing with things that we may not understand.

Koichi Kawakita replaced Teruyoshi Nakano as Special Effects Director, and not only created a new Godzilla suit that would allow for better maneuverability, but also added intimidating touches like extra rows of teeth, and removed the whites of Godzilla's eyes. The Biollante suits were feats of engineering themselves, the final form especially proving a challenge as over 30 wires were required to puppeteer Biollante's many tentacles, and took hours to set up.

Godzilla vs. Biollante stands out as one of the most unique entries in the Godzilla franchise, as well as one of its most melancholy. Despite finding critical success, the mature themes and bizarre nature of the plot didn't sit as well with audiences, and it was considered a disappointment at the box office. Toho would return with another adventure for Godzilla only two years later, this time with one of the most fantastical storylines of the entire franchise, as well as a fan-favorite foe for Godzilla to battle...

Previous page (left): Godzilla at home in the water.

Previous page (right): Another look at Godzilla's updated design.

Above left: Biollante with her many rows of teeth.

Above right: Flowers, this film's symbol of love, loss, remembrance, and beauty.

Left: Godzilla in danger of Biollante's gaping maw.

Opposite: Biollante seeming to wear a sinister smile.

ゴジラvsキングギドラ

GODZILLA VS. KING GHIDORAH (1991)

DIRECTOR : KAZUKI OHMORI
WRITTEN BY : KAZUKI OHMORI
PRODUCED BY : SHOGO TOMIYAMA
SPECIAL EFFECTS DIRECTOR : KOWICHI KAWAKITA
SCORE : AKIRA IFUKUBE
STARRING : KOSUKE TOYOHARA, ANNA NAKAGAWA, MEGUMI ODAKA, KATSUHIKO SASAKI, AKIJI KOBAYASHI, KENPACHIRO SATSUMA

IN THE WAKE OF A DISAPPOINTING BOX OFFICE RETURN FOR *GODZILLA VS. BIOLLANTE*, PRODUCERS POINTED TO A FEW POTENTIAL CULPRITS: A PLOT TOO COMPLICATED FOR CHILDREN TO FOLLOW, DARK THEMES THAT WERE BETTER SUITED TO ADULTS THAN CHILDREN, AND BOX OFFICE COMPETITION WITH THE MONUMENTALLY POPULAR *BACK TO THE FUTURE PART II*.

As a result, the decision was made to lighten the material for a younger audience, re-introduce one of Godzilla's most famous antagonists in King Ghidorah, and include time travel as a story element.

And so, *Godzilla vs. King Ghidorah* was born. Set in the far future 2204 AD, a group of explorers discovers the dead body of King Ghidorah at the bottom of the ocean, minus one of its three heads. We learn that in the distant past, Godzilla fought and destroyed King Ghidorah in an epic battle. We then jump to the present day, 1992, in Japan, where a science fiction author is researching stories of a dinosaur on an island in the South Pacific that purportedly saved a group of Japanese soldiers during the Second World War. He hypothesizes that this dinosaur must have been irradiated by the H-bomb test in 1954, and had mutated into Godzilla. A wealthy businessman, Yasuaki Shindo, had been one of the soldiers on that island and confirmed that yes, the dinosaur had indeed existed.

And then, a UFO arrives at Mount Fuji! The inhabitants of the UFO are the Futurians, a trio of time travelers (plus their trusty android) from the far future who have bad news for present day Japan.

It seems that at some point during the course of history, Godzilla ravages Japan and completely eradicates it from the globe. They have come back in time to warn Japan of this, in the hopes of altering history so that Godzilla can be destroyed before it has the chance to destroy Japan once and for all. Their plan is to take a small crew to 1944, to the small island where the mysterious dinosaur had saved that group of Japanese soldiers, and move the dinosaur so that it will not be irradiated by the H-bomb. If they succeed in their plan, Godzilla will never exist!

Psychic Miki from the previous film joins the small team as they go to war-ravaged 1944 and witness a harrowing battle between the American forces and the dinosaur, which the Americans mortally wound. The Futurians then teleport the wounded dinosaur to the bottom of the Bering Strait, far from the blast zone of the H-bomb, ensuring that Godzilla is erased from history.

But before they leave 1944, one of the Futurians secretly releases three tiny, cute, winged creatures on the island – creatures with a strangely familiar golden, scaly sheen...

Back in 1992, it is confirmed that indeed Godzilla has never existed... however, a new monster has taken its place: King Ghidorah! The Futurians have double-crossed Japan – apparently in the far future, Japan is actually the greatest superpower the world has ever known, and the Futurians hoped to destroy Japan so that in their time the other nations of the world would gain more power. Knowing Godzilla to be a protector, they eliminated the monster from history and created King Ghidorah. Unchecked, with no other monsters to defy it, King Ghidorah is on a nonstop rampage of destruction across Japan.

A plan is hatched to find the long-dead dinosaur at the bottom of the Bering Strait and use a nuclear warhead to revive and mutate it. The plan works, and Godzilla has returned once more to battle King Ghidorah to the death.

But there's yet one more twist. Upon destroying King Ghidorah, Godzilla then turns its attention on Tokyo, cutting its own swath of mayhem. The sole surviving Futurian – a kind one on the side of humanity – travels into the future and returns moments later with... Mecha-King Ghidorah!

Now it is up to Emmy (our Futurian friend) and her remote-controlled Mecha-King Ghidorah to repel Godzilla and bring safety and peace to Japan once again.

This would be the first film in the series not produced by franchise

お前だけには絶対負けない！
世紀末・最大の戦いが始まった。
ゴジラ
VS
キングギドラ
製作■田中友幸　脚本・監督■大森一樹　特技監督■川北紘一　音楽監督■伊福部 昭
中川安奈○豊原功補○小高恵美/原田貴和子/佐々木勝彦/チャック・ウィルソン○山村 聡○小林昭二/上田耕一/リチャード・バーガー/ロバート・スコットフィールド○西岡徳馬○土屋嘉男
©1991 TOHO
サントラ盤●バンダイビジュアル/製作●東宝映画/配給●東宝 DOLBY STEREO
阪急東宝グループ

creator Tomoyuki Tanaka, who had to leave the project due to ailing health. Returning for the first time since the Showa Era, however, was original composer Akira Ifukube, delivering his iconic themes in an all-new, bombastic score.

The film faced a certain amount of controversy upon its release in America, as many felt that the scene in which the dinosaur obliterates the American forces was too anti-American. Tensions were particularly high during this period of time between the US and Japan, and director Kazuki Omori stated there was no such anti-American sentiment intended, supposing that the political climate contributed to people finding subtext where none existed.

Controversy aside, *Godzilla vs. King Ghidorah* is a fantastical, fun, loud, raucous adventure into the far future and the not-so-distant past, and proved that Godzilla could be both exciting for adults and entertaining for children as well. The next year, Toho would follow this same formula, bringing back another kaiju from its famous roster, one that had been both friend and foe to Godzilla in the past...

Top: King Ghidorah, unleashed upon the world once more.

Above: The dead dinosaur killed by soldiers during the Second World War.

Opposite: The Godzillasaurus that became Godzilla, and before the time travelers meddled in history.

Left: Mecha-King Ghidorah battling Godzilla.

Top: The reveal of the terrifying Mecha-King Ghidorah.

Middle: One of the small creatures released by the Futurians.

Above: Godzilla locked in battle with King Ghidorah's many heads.

ゴジラvsモスラ

GODZILLA VS. MOTHRA (1992)

DIRECTOR : TAKAO OKAWARA
WRITTEN BY : KAZUKI OHMORI
PRODUCED BY : SHOGO TOMIYAMA
SPECIAL EFFECTS DIRECTOR : KOWICHI KAWAKITA
SCORE : AKIRA IFUKUBE
STARRING : TETSUYA BESSHO, SATOMI KOBAYASHI, TAKEHIRO MURATA, SABURO SHINODA, AKIJI KOBAYASHI, MEGUMI ODAKA, KENPACHIRO SATSUMA

ALSO KNOWN AS *GODZILLA AND MOTHRA: THE BATTLE FOR EARTH*, THIS 19TH FILM IN THE FRANCHISE RE-INTRODUCES A FRIENDLY FACE IN MOTHRA AND LEANS MORE HEAVILY INTO THE FAMILY-FRIENDLY, FANTASY SETTING THAT THE SHOWA ERA WAS KNOWN FOR.

Following the pattern established here in the Heisei Era, Godzilla is once again an aggressor – a being to be feared by humanity.

The film opens with a meteor crashing to earth, causing landslides on faraway Infant Island (a name that should be familiar to Godzilla fans), and uncovering what appears to be a gigantic egg...

Meanwhile, an Indiana Jones-like explorer is in the midst of a daring escape from a crumbling temple, having looted a valuable artifact. Upon his return to the surface, he is immediately captured by the authorities and given an offer he can't refuse: go to jail, or travel to Infant Island to solve an archaeological mystery. Not only must he go on this new expedition, but he is being paired with his ex-wife on the team!

Once at the island, they uncover ancient cave drawings that seem to depict two insects in battle, and also the giant egg that appears to be intact. They meet the Cosmos – the Heisei Era's name for the tiny Shobijin twins that communicate with Mothra – and learn that in ancient times an evil mirror of Mothra was created when man began destroying the planet. See, thousands of years ago there was an advanced civilization not unlike our own, but man's tendency to destroy the planet through greed and pollution was true even then, and born of that waste was Battra, a destructive opposite of Mothra that vowed to destroy humanity for what it had done to Earth.

Mothra defeated Battra way back then, but seeing as how the meteor unearthed Mothra's egg, the Cosmos fear that Battra too would have been awakened. Battra would know that humanity has not ceased destroying the planet, and so would return to its rampage of calamity around the globe.

In addition, that same meteor also awoke Godzilla!

Soon, Godzilla discovers Mothra's egg, which hatches, and does battle with the larval form of Mothra. Battra (also in larval form, although with a giant electricity-spewing horn atop its head) tracks them down mid-battle, and all three fight in the open ocean.

The power of the skirmish opens a rift in the sea floor that appears to consume Godzilla and Battra, and Mothra heads for Japan in pursuit of its tiny friends the Cosmos.

Larval Mothra uncharacteristically destroys the city as she looks for the Cosmos (who have been kidnapped by an evil corporation, naturally), but eventually stops when she knows they are safe. It is time now for her to cocoon, in the middle of the city.

While she rests, Godzilla reappears and begins to wreak havoc, unchecked and unstoppable, but not for long! Not only does Mothra emerge from her cocoon now in her final winged form, but Battra too has evolved and sprouted sharp leathery wings! The two former rivals team up against Godzilla. This leads to a massive, final nighttime battle at a Yokohama amusement park, with both Mothra and Battra unleashing a battery of energy blasts, electricity, snapping mandibles, and magical hypnotic dust.

The end of the film is a warning to humanity, in its own way. We learn that a meteor is coming to Earth, and will destroy humanity in 1999. Mothra is going to attempt to steer it away on behalf of the planet, a sobering reminder that we must be grateful to the planet for her protection, and remember that the more we destroy, the less of a home we're going to have.

"THE POWER OF THE SKIRMISH OPENS A RIFT IN THE SEA FLOOR THAT APPEARS TO CONSUME GODZILLA AND BATTRA, AND MOTHRA HEADS FOR JAPAN IN PURSUIT OF ITS TINY FRIENDS THE COSMOS."

極彩色の大決戦！

ゴジラ vs モスラ

GODZILLA vs MOTHRA

地球SOS！人類の未来をかけた戦いが始まる。

製作■田中友幸　脚本■大森一樹　音楽監督■伊福部 昭　特技監督■川北紘一　監督■大河原孝夫

別所哲也○小林聡美○村田雄浩/小高恵美○米澤史織(子役)/大竹まこと○小林昭二○上田耕一○大和田伸也/今村恵子○大沢さやか/篠田三郎○宝田 明

主題歌「モスラの歌」(東芝EMI)/協賛●WOWOW日本衛星放送㈱・㈱ナムコ・コニカ㈱・㈱西友/製作●東宝映画/配給●東宝　DOLBY STEREO　©1992 TOHO

阪急東宝グループ

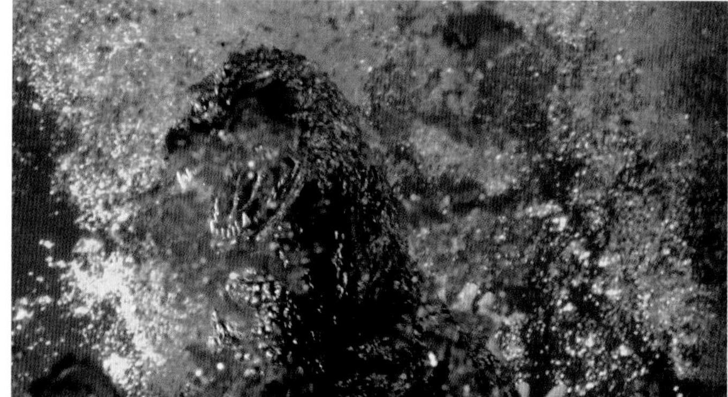

The film treats Mothra with a tremendous amount of mythic respect, her original theme and the song of the Cosmos both comforting and iconic. It also characterizes her magic as ancient and elegant, with a seriousness that's neither silly nor dour. Perhaps more than any other film in the franchise, Mothra here is treated as truly a goddess. She is Mother Earth.

Godzilla vs. Mothra would be the final Godzilla set on which franchise father Ishiro Honda would set foot. He visited the set shortly before passing away at age 81.

The next film in the franchise was originally intended to be the last, in part to honor the upcoming 40th anniversary of Godzilla. They would follow the form of the previous two films by resurrecting another age-old foe, a familiar face to fans, and an adversary that Godzilla had battled multiple times before...

Top: Battra descending on Tokyo Harbor.

Above (left): Mothra after having cocooned the Diet Building.

Above (right): Godzilla in watery fury.

Opposite: The final battle where two foes unite to take on Godzilla.

ゴジラvsメカゴジラ

GODZILLA VS. MECHAGODZILLA II (1993)

DIRECTOR : TAKAO OKAWARA
WRITTEN BY : WATARU MIMURA
PRODUCED BY : SHOGO TOMIYAMA
SPECIAL EFFECTS DIRECTOR : KOWICHI KAWAKITA
SCORE : AKIRA IFUKUBE
STARRING : MASAHIRO TAKASHIMA, RYOKO SANO, MEGUMI ODAKA, YUSUKE KAWAZU, AKIRA NAKAO, KENPACHIRO SATSUMA, WATARU FUKUDA, HURRICANE RYU

FOLLOWING THE POPULARITY OF BRINGING BACK FAMILIAR MONSTERS FROM THE SHOWA ERA IN *GODZILLA VS. KING GHIDORAH* AND *GODZILLA VS. MOTHRA*, TOHO RESURRECTED ANOTHER LEGENDARY ADVERSARY TO THE KING OF THE MONSTERS, MECHAGODZILLA.

This time, however, it would not be operated by aliens seeking to take over the world, but instead by the newly-formed G-Force, a human-led military organization dedicated to defeating Godzilla once and for all.

Following the events of *Godzilla vs. King Ghidorah*, G-Force salvages the robotic head of Mecha-King Ghidorah that had been built in the future, reverse engineering the technology to create two new Godzilla-killing weapons. First is the Garuda, a high-tech flying tank capable of powerful energy blasts, and the second is of course the all-new Mechagodzilla, a huge mecha piloted by elite commandos in its head.

Meanwhile, an exploratory mission to radioactive Adona Island uncovers a giant un-hatched egg, which appears to be that of a pteranodon. As the team attempts to take the egg with them back to the mainland, a furious Rodan awakens and attacks them, the noise of which then summons Godzilla from the waves, and the two engage in epic battle. Throughout the humans' escape with their prize, the egg seems to pulsate in response to the presence of the young female researcher.

Back in Kyoto, the egg suddenly hatches, and a Baby Godzilla emerges. It appears to be peaceful, as well as a vegetarian. Further, it has imprinted on the same female scientist that it had reacted to psychically while still in the egg. For all intents and purposes, she is the baby's mother.

"G-FORCE SALVAGES THE ROBOTIC HEAD OF MECHA-KING GHIDORAH... REVERSE ENGINEERING THE TECHNOLOGY TO CREATE TWO NEW GODZILLA-KILLING WEAPONS."

Godzilla appears to psychically sense Baby Godzilla, and so follows it to the mainland, unleashing chaos as it destroys the city looking for its offspring. The scientists whisk the baby away to a safe house while Godzilla continues to destroy Kyoto. Fortunately, G-Force has Mechagodzilla ready for battle, and a huge showdown occurs between the two. After a lengthy – and frequently bloody – fight, Godzilla ends up disabling Mechagodzilla and retreats to the sea... for now.

Eventually, the team discovers a weakness in Godzilla – as well as a psychic link between Godzilla and the child (thanks to psychic Heisei mainstay Miki Saegusa) – and a final battle occurs between Godzilla, Rodan, Mechagodzilla, and the airborne Garuda. A shocking self-sacrifice from Rodan, and an all-new, unexpected transformation on the part of Mechagodzilla lead to the ultimate climax, in which Godzilla and Baby Godzilla – now father and son – are reunited, and the future appears bright for the monstrous pair.

This film was intended to be the final film of the Heisei Era, to honor the recent passing of Ishiro Honda and to avoid competing with the Americans' impending remake. With this being the intended farewell, Toho wanted to bring back not only one of Godzilla's most famous enemies, but also one of the franchise's cutest creations, Minilla. Here called Baby Godzilla, the youngster brings an all-new levity to the hitherto more serious Heisei Era, and helps to humanize Godzilla by the end of the film in a touching way that echoes the evolution in the Showa Era of Godzilla as destructor to Godzilla as ally. *Godzilla vs. Mechagodzilla II* (which despite its name is not a direct sequel to the original *Godzilla vs. Mechagodzilla*) manages to walk the tightrope that is balancing the Heisei Era's adult-oriented seriousness and action film bombast, with the childlike awe and softness of the mid-to-late Showa Era. The final moments with Baby Godzilla are some of the most heartfelt – and heartbreaking – moments of the entire franchise.

世紀末覇王誕生。
だれもがこの戦いを待っていた。
ゴジラ VS メカゴジラ
ベビーGをめぐる、
史上最大の三大バトルが始まる!
製作■田中友幸 プロデューサー■富山省吾 脚本■三村 渉 音楽監督■伊福部 昭 特技監督■川北紘一 監督■大河原孝夫
高嶋政宏 佐野量子 小高恵美 原田大二郎 宮川一朗太 佐原健二 ラサール石井 高島忠夫(特別出演) 中尾 彬 川津祐介
協賛■株日本旅行 コニカ株 株西友 製作■東宝映画 配給■東宝 ©1993 TOHO
40th

Akira Ifukube provided a huge score that weaved new themes with recognizable, classic ones. The music is loud and triumphant, as well as tender and gentle, a mirror of this film's celebration of military might combined with the innocence of Baby Godzilla's birth and struggle.

Featuring some of the most action-packed monster battles of the entire franchise, *Godzilla vs. Mechagodzilla II* proved to be so entertaining that there was no way it would be the final entry of the Heisei Era. In fact, an all-new monster was waiting in the wings, one with an instantly iconic design that is both beautiful and deadly.

The Heisei Mechagodzilla may not have come from the stars, but Godzilla's newest adversary would come speeding down from the endless void of space...

Opposite: The Heisei Era's new version of Minilla.

Above: Three familiar foes in three new iterations.

Left: The crew prepares the city for Mechagodzilla's arrival.

Opposite: A new and improved Super Mechagodzilla.

Right: Godzilla, larger and more imposing than ever before.

ゴジラvsスペースゴジラ

GODZILLA VS. SPACEGODZILLA (1994)

DIRECTOR : KENSHO YAMASHITA
WRITTEN BY : KANJI KASHIWA, HIROSHI KASHIWABARA
PRODUCED BY : SHOGO TOMIYAMA
SPECIAL EFFECTS DIRECTOR : KOWICHI KAWAKITA
SCORE : TAKAYUKI HATTORI
STARRING : MEGUMI ODAKA, JUN HASHIZUME, ZENKICHI YONEYAMA, AKIRA EMOTO, TOWAKO YOSHIKAWA, KENPACHIRO SATSUMA, LITTLE FRANKIE, RYO HARITANI, WATARU FUKUDA

GIGANTIC MAGIC CRYSTALS, TELEKINETIC KAIJU, PSYCHIC WARNINGS FROM AN INTERSTELLAR MOTHRA, HUGE MULTI-FORM BATTLE MECHAS, AND A BEAST BORN IN A BLACK HOLE – THESE ARE THE ELEMENTS OF THIS MEGA-SIZED ENTRY IN THE GODZILLA FRANCHISE.

It is a heavily science fiction adventure that in addition to the above features a rogue soldier seeking to kill Godzilla himself, a Yakuza kidnapping and daring rescue, and even Little Godzilla (no longer a baby) learning how to use its heat ray powers.

Godzilla vs. SpaceGodzilla opens with a massive crystalline object hurling through space, destroying a NASA space station and eventually slamming into the earth, forming a bizarre "palace" of giant crystals teeming with energy.

Meanwhile, the government is about to unleash its latest attempt to eliminate Godzilla, the new battlemech known as M.O.G.U.E.R.A. – sort of a Mechagodzilla 2.0, complete with detachable sections and enormous drills. At the same time, an attempt is being made to use psychic Miki Saegusa (returning yet again to the franchise after featuring in every film since *Godzilla vs. Biollante*) to commune with Godzilla and hopefully figure out how to control it. In the midst of this experiment, Mothra (and the tiny Cosmos) appear to Miki and warn her of the impending danger of SpaceGodzilla.

And a danger it is. Created when Godzilla's cells (borne to space by Mothra at the end of *Godzilla vs. Mothra*) journeyed through a black hole, SpaceGodzilla is a massive copy of Godzilla, except with telekinetic powers and huge amounts of energy pulsing from enormous crystals embedded in its back.

SpaceGodzilla attacks Godzilla and Little Godzilla (who has grown substantially since we last saw it) and proves a more than formidable foe. It traps Little Godzilla in a crystalline prison and then heads straight for Tokyo!

The battle then rages as Godzilla and SpaceGodzilla take part in a psychedelic clash of colors and high-flying acrobatics, with SpaceGodzilla able to lift Godzilla into the air and fling it across the city. M.O.G.U.E.R.A. is activated and joins the assault, teaming up with Godzilla against the greater threat.

Godzilla vs. SpaceGodzilla was directed by Kensho Yamashita. His background directing teen idol films clearly influenced the frenzied, lighthearted sensibilities of this movie. Design influences came from video games, and the inclusion of M.O.G.U.E.R.A. would have been thrilling for fans of Ishiro Honda's 1950s sci-fi classic *The Mysterians*, from which the mecha originated and hadn't been seen in decades.

The monster battles in this film are particularly spectacular, and are without a doubt the standout of this entry in the franchise. A tremendous amount of wirework was required to lift the massive monster suits, and the addition of huge explosions and falling stalactite-like crystals make for a maelstrom of action in the lengthy final act (which is almost entirely one long battle) of the film.

In addition, recurring character Miki Saegusa, the psychic who can communicate with Godzilla, has her largest role of any of the Heisei Era films here. While she has played an integral role in the previous entries, here she is the sole advocate for Godzilla. She pleads with the multitude of characters seeking to destroy it to

Left: Spacegodzilla amidst its Crystal Palace.

破壊神降臨

G細胞×ブラックホール　究極の戦闘生物が誕生した

ゴジラVSスペースゴジラ

製作■田中友幸／協同製作■富山省吾／脚本■柏原寛司
特技監督■川北紘一／監督■山下賢章
音楽■服部隆之／主題歌■デイト・オブ・バース(キティエンタープライズ)
橋爪 淳／小高恵美／米山善吉／中尾 彬 斉藤洋介 佐原健二
今村恵子・大沢さやか(コスモス)／吉川十和子／柄本 明

撮影■岸本正広／美術■酒井 賢／録音■宮内一男／照明■望月英樹／編集■米田美保
助監督■三好邦夫／製作補■有正真一郎 製作担当者■徳増俊郎
(特殊技術)
撮影■江口憲一・大川藤雄／美術■大澤哲三／照明■斉藤 薫／操演■小川昭二・金子久夫
特殊効果■渡辺忠昭／造型■小林知己／助監督■鈴木健二／製作担当者■小島太郎
協賛■西友・JOMO・コニカ／製作■東宝映画／配給■東宝

200695-215

©1994 TOHO

understand that Godzilla has thoughts and feelings just like all of us and that the answer to conflict is not simply to fight about it. This proves to be perhaps the strongest theme of this film in particular, that while sometimes we must fight, it is equally important to search for peaceful ways to resolve a conflict. By the end, when not only has Godzilla worked with the humans inside M.O.G.U.E.R.A. to defeat SpaceGodzilla, we also see that Little Godzilla is once again safe and sound, and learning how to breathe its own heat ray. As a mercenary (and longtime nemesis of Godzilla) says, "maybe Godzilla's not so bad a creature."

The next year, Toho would revive Godzilla one final time in the Heisei Era, bringing to a conclusion one of the franchise's most cohesive story arcs, but also potentially ending the entire franchise as a whole. Audiences knew that there was a very real possibility that this next film would be Godzilla's last...

Opposite (top left): Little Godzilla, always in grave danger in this film.

Opposite (top right): Godzilla helping teach Little Godzilla how to protect itself.

Opposite: Godzilla and Spacegodzilla face off amidst a forest of deadly crystals.

Above: Behind the scenes photo of the three main kaiju about to shoot another battle scene.

ゴジラvsスペースゴジラ

GODZILLA VS. DESTOROYAH (1995)

DIRECTOR : TAKAO OKAWARA
WRITTEN BY : KAZUKI OHMORI
PRODUCED BY : SHOGO TOMIYAMA
SPECIAL EFFECTS DIRECTOR : KOWICHI KAWAKITA
SCORE : AKIRA IFUKUBE
STARRING : TAKURO TATSUMI, YOKO ISHINO, MEGUMI ODAKA, YASUFUMI HAYASHI, SAYAKA OSAWA, MOMOKO KOCHI, KENPACHIRO SATSUMA, RYO HARIYA, EIICHI YANAGIDA, HURRICANE RYU.

"THE DEATH OF GODZILLA" THAT'S HOW *GODZILLA VS. DESTOROYAH* – ITSELF THE FILM THAT WOULD MARK THE 40TH ANNIVERSARY OF THE ORIGINAL FILM – WAS MARKETED TO MOVIEGOERS EXCITED ABOUT GODZILLA'S NEXT OUTING.

Godzilla's final film in the Heisei Era would not only have it squaring off against one of its largest and most terrifying foes yet, it would also be one of the most purely tragic and heartbreaking of the entire series. Not a dry eye would remain by the end of this film, and Godzilla itself would never be the same...

Psychic Miki Saegusa returns to Birth Island, where we had last seen Godzilla and Little Godzilla, to check up on their status. Upon arrival, however, she finds the entire island to have been destroyed, and both of the kaiju missing! It's discovered that due to a freak occurrence, some kind of natural nuclear explosion in the earth must have destroyed the island, taking both Godzilla and its son with it.

Soon after, however, Godzilla emerges from the sea – it may be alive, but in no form we've ever seen it. The monster is glowing red, with its nuclear-like heart overflowing with energy, and a body temperature that is rising daily. Gozilla seeks out nuclear power plants from which it can feed, because its heart is consuming so much energy.

Meanwhile, a young amateur scientist – the grandson of the original film's Dr. Yamane (the pacifist scientist who sought to study Godzilla rather than destroy the creature) – theorizes that Godzilla's heart will explode if it reaches 1200 degrees. And when that happens, it would have the collective power of every nuclear weapon on Earth. It will, he says, burn the atmosphere and wipe out all life on the planet. Conventional weapons might detonate Godzilla prematurely, so he suggests the only solution might be Dr. Serizawa's Oxygen Destroyer from the first film, if they can recreate it. This of course is deeply troubling to his aunt, the original film's Emiko Yamane (here reprised by the original actress Momoko Kochi, her final role before her passing). We recall that Emiko was engaged to Dr Serizawa, and she above all understood his torment over his creation, and the gravity of his sacrifice to keep it from being used ever again.

Amidst all of this, another scientist has salvaged geologic samples from Tokyo Bay, particles that appear to have been created when the original Oxygen Destroyer was used in 1954. Through his experiments, he finds that some of these particles have come to life, and have escaped his lab. Soon, all the fish in the neighboring aquarium have disintegrated, in an alarmingly similar way to how the Oxygen Destroyer works.

Soon, these Oxygen Destroyer (known as Destoroyah) particles mutate and evolve into ever-larger monsters, and in a number of scenes straight out of a horror film, soldiers attempt to subdue them to little effect. The creatures grow and grow, and soon there is one large Destroyer on the rampage.

To Miki's great relief, Little Godzilla (now dubbed Junior) has emerged safely from the sea, unharmed, and is attempting to return to its original home on Adonoa Island. Godzilla – still on the verge of a world-ending meltdown – is following its son to peace and safety. With Destoroyah on the loose, however, the government convinces a tormented Miki to use her psychic powers to lure Junior, and therefore Godzilla, back to Tokyo so that Godzilla can battle Destoroyah. Essentially, using Junior as bait. She struggled with this moral quandary but ultimately knows that without Godzilla there to protect them, Japan will be lost to Destoroyah.

When all three monsters finally meet, deep and harrowing tragedy strikes when Destoroyah violently kills Junior, and Godzilla unleashes all of its rage and sadness at the loss of its son. It's a massive battle between two true titans, with the loss of the innocent child at the center.

By the end, we are left with a collective cheer of triumph, the pain of loss, a gratitude for Godzilla's legacy as both villain and protector, and hope for new beginnings in the series. The Heisei Era's seven-film canonical arc reaches its conclusion, and a familiar roar fills the sky above a ruined Tokyo.

In a fitting tribute, composer Akira Ifukube would craft this as

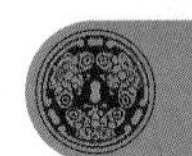

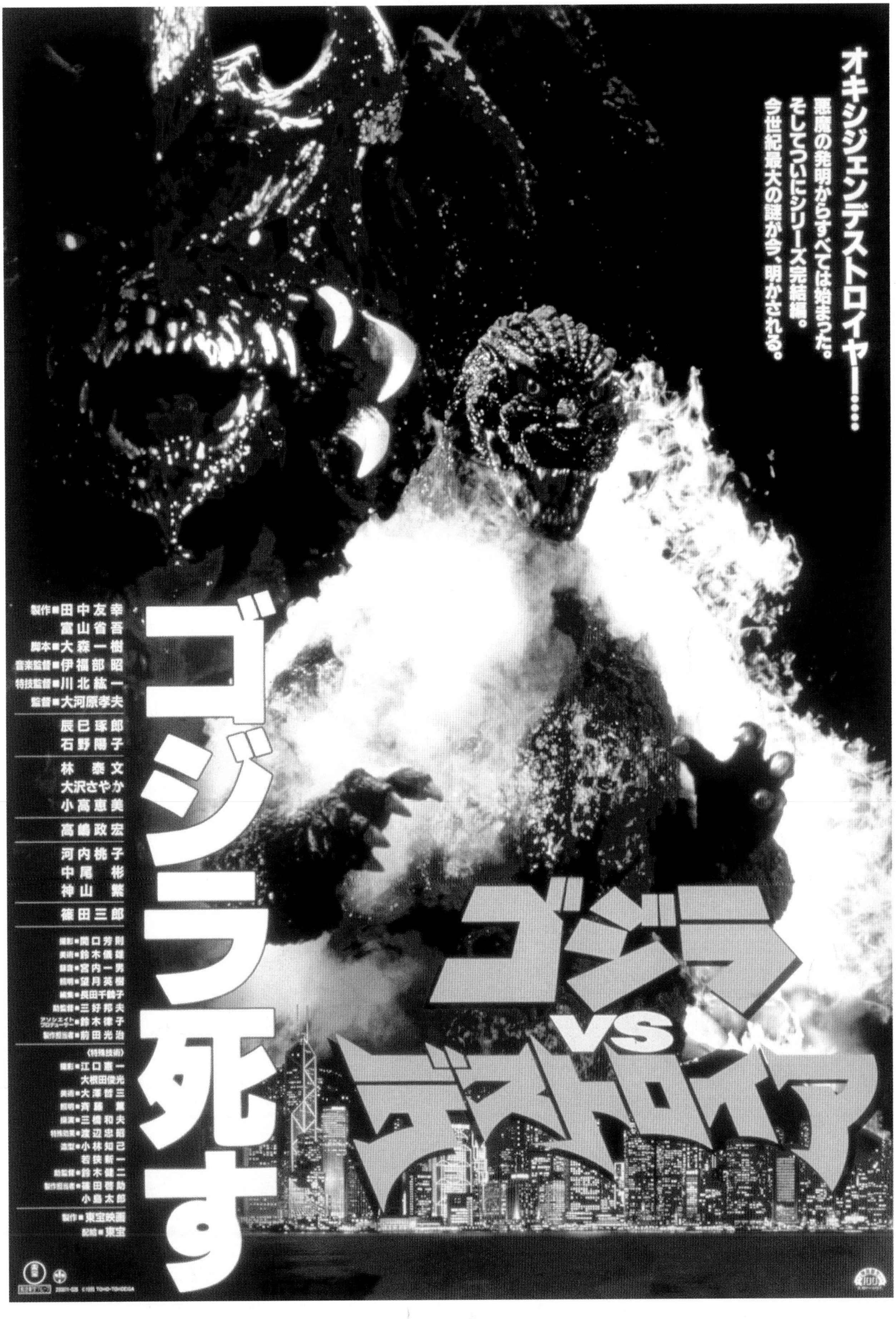
オキシジェンデストロイヤー……
悪魔の発明からすべては始まった。
そしてついにシリーズ完結編。
今世紀最大の謎が今、明かされる。
ゴジラ死す
ゴジラ VS デストロイア
製作■田中友幸
富山省吾
脚本■大森一樹
音楽監督■伊福部昭
特技監督■川北紘一
監督■大河原孝夫
辰巳琢郎
石野陽子
林泰文
大沢さやか
小高恵美
高嶋政宏
河内桃子
中尾彬
神山繁
篠田三郎
撮影■関口芳則
美術■鈴木儀雄
録音■宮内一男
照明■望月英樹
編集■長田千鶴子
助監督■三好邦夫
アソシエイトプロデューサー■鈴木律子
製作担当者■前田光治
《特殊技術》
撮影■江口憲一
大根田俊光
美術■大澤哲三
照明■斉藤薫
操演■三橋和夫
特殊効果■渡辺忠昭
造型■小林知己
若狭新一
助監督■鈴木健二
製作担当者■篠田啓助
小島太郎
製作■東宝映画
配給■東宝
© 1995 TOHO-TOHOEIGA

his final score for the Godzilla franchise. He said that he felt it was appropriate, as since he had "been involved in Godzilla's birth, it was fitting for [him] to be involved in its death". The final moments of the score in particular serve not only as a funereal dirge for Godzilla the monster, but for the franchise as a whole.

There's a deep and enduring sadness that permeates this film, but not without an equally powerful sense of pride and honor. Here we have Godzilla as a ticking time bomb, but not due to anger or a desire to commit violence. Instead, for the first time, Godzilla is subject to forces beyond even its control. And amidst this pain and uncertainty, its instinct to protect (and then, tragically, mourn and avenge) its son drives it ever forward.

In an echo to the original film, the human characters are far more flawed than the monsters, but as with the original film their struggles are also layered and complex. In the first film they understand the danger of using the Oxygen Destroyer, but know that they must if they are going to save the people of Japan. Similarly, Miki's decision to guide Junior back to Tokyo signs its death warrant, but it arguably saves the planet. It is a film filled with devil's bargains, and points out the folly of man, the inherent humanity of all living things, and the impossible choices that sometimes must be made for the common good.

There's a lot to unpack in *Godzilla vs. Destoroyah*, and it served as a respectful – however heartrending – end to Godzilla itself and to the Heisei Era. Godzilla fans wept along with Miki Saegusa as she said through tears at the end of the film, "My work with Godzilla has finished."

Audiences would only have to wait five short years, however, before Godzilla would re-emerge in Japan to usher in the new millennium...

Above: Destoroyah looming over the city.

Right: Destoroyah's horrifying - and gigantic - final form.

Opposite: The updated design for Godzilla 1995.

Top: Godzilla Junior arriving to do battle.

Above: A near-nuclear Godzilla facing off with a seemingly unstoppable Destoroyah.

Right: Behind-the-scenes shot of Godzilla's final on-screen moment.

ミレニアムシリーズ

MILLENNIUM ERA

Toho inaugurated the new millennium by resurrecting Godzilla for a whole new era, one that would be defined by explosive special effects, a focus on monsters from films past, and an anthology style that saw each film exist in its own continuity, separate from each other. This allowed the filmmakers to explore more disparate themes without being hindered by a need to adhere to plot carrying over from the films that came before, and resulted in a run of six films that are each wildly different, but equally as powerful in their individual messages and themes. The Millennium Era ran from 1999 until Godzilla's 50th anniversary in 2004, and offered fans perhaps the most diverse and adventurous era in the franchise's history.

THE MILLENNIUM ERA FILMS ARE:

GODZILLA 2000: MILLENNIUM (1999) • GODZILLA VS. MEGAGUIRUS (2000)
GODZILLA, MOTHRA AND KING GHIDORAH: GIANT MONSTERS ALL-OUT ATTACK (2001)
GODZILLA AGAINST MECHAGODZILLA (2002) • GODZILLA: TOKYO S.O.S. (2003)
GODZILLA: FINAL WARS (2004)

ゴジラ2000 ミレニアム

GODZILLA 2000: MILLENNIUM (1999)

DIRECTOR : TAKAO OKAWARA
WRITTEN BY : HIROSHI KASHIWABARA, WATARU MIMURA
PRODUCED BY : SHOGO TOMIYAMA
SPECIAL EFFECTS DIRECTOR : KENJI SUZUKI
SCORE : TAKAYUKI HATTORI
STARRING : TAKEHIRO MURATA, HIROSHI ABE, NAOMI NISHIDA, MAYU SUZUKI, SHIRO SANO, TSUTOMU KITAGAWA, MAKOTO ITO

AFTER A BRIEF FIVE YEAR HIATUS, TOHO KNEW THE BEST WAY TO USHER IN A NEW MILLENNIUM WOULD BE WITH A NEW ERA OF GODZILLA FILMS. THUS, *GODZILLA 2000: MILLENNIUM* WAS BORN.

It would set the tone for the Millennium Era, featuring sci-fi plots and fast-paced action, as well as utilizing state-of-the-art computer-generated effects more than ever before. It was truly Godzilla for a new age.

The overall arc of the franchise is yet again reset, this installment functioning as a sequel of sorts to the 1954 original. Here, the Godzilla Protection Network (or GPN) works to track and predict where Godzilla might surface, and when it might strike again. Godzilla arrives at the top of the film – newly designed with aggressive razor-sharp teeth and elongated, claw-like spines along its back – and begins to destroy a small village.

Meanwhile, a 60-million-year-old UFO is discovered at the bottom of the ocean, and as scientists attempt to raise it for study, it suddenly takes off of its own accord and flies straight for Godzilla!

After a brief battle in which the UFO is able to drive Godzilla away, it lands atop a tower in the center of Tokyo where it proceeds to siphon information from the tower's supercomputers, absorbing all the knowledge contained within! Soon, the UFO broadcasts a signal: it intends to take over the world.

The military attempts to destroy the UFO with explosive charges, but to no avail. What's more, the GPN has ascertained that the UFO was searching the computers for information regarding Godzilla's DNA, specifically its regenerative capabilities. It would appear the aliens hope to use this DNA to remake themselves in Godzilla's image.

Soon, Godzilla arrives and does battle once again with the UFO – but the UFO has used some of its newly-gained Godzilla DNA to evolve into a number of new forms, each larger and more terrifying than the last. In its final form – known as Orga – it puts up a respectable fight against Godzilla, at one point attempting to swallow the King of the Monsters whole. It's truly epic and leads to a climax befitting of the rebirth of cinema's greatest monster.

Godzilla 2000: Millennium was announced relatively quickly following the premiere of Roland Emmerich's 1998 *Godzilla* reboot in America. After taking the character in such a different direction, fans were eager for a return to form, and for Toho to be at the helm. The writers of *Godzilla vs. Mechagodzilla II* and *Godzilla vs. SpaceGodzilla* returned to pen the screenplay, hoping to examine the core of what makes Godzilla so special and enduring.

The design of the new millennium's Godzilla would be shorter than that of the Heisei, with director Takao Okawara hoping to make it a closer, more immediate threat to the humans, as opposed to a towering behemoth that you couldn't look in the eye. He utilizes this to great effect when at the end of the film Godzilla is able to do just that with his human rival, the head of the GPN who has been hunting it for years. This personal connection between man and monster bridges the gap of the anthropomorphized Godzilla of the Showa Era with the pure force of nature of the original film.

"FEATURING SCI-FI PLOTS AND FAST-PACED ACTION, AS WELL AS UTILIZING STATE-OF-THE-ART COMPUTER-GENERATED EFFECTS MORE THAN EVER BEFORE. IT WAS TRULY GODZILLA FOR A NEW AGE."

目撃せよ！ゴジラ新世紀
延べ9,000万人が観た映画史上最強シリーズ。沈黙を破り、世紀末日本に新破壊神伝説が始動する。
12月11日(土)全国東宝系公開
ゴジラ
2000
ミレニアム
村田雄浩　阿部寛　西田尚美　鈴木麻由　佐野史郎
製作／富山省吾　脚本／柏原寛司・三村渉　特殊技術／鈴木健二　監督／大河原孝夫
製作／東宝映画　配給／東宝
www.godzilla.co.jp

The tone also finds a balance between serious monster action and light-hearted fun, with some truly terrifying and awe-inspiring visions of Godzilla's destruction juxtaposed with moments of people hilariously barely avoiding getting killed. It's a tone that finds DNA in the family-friendly Showa Era and the more serious Heisei: this is Godzilla through and through.

The very next year, Godzilla would return with another film that yet again resets the continuity to ignore all but Ishiro Honda's 1954 classic, a film that will once again pit the King of the Monsters against a new foe and return the franchise to the monster-on-monster action it is known for...

Opposite: Costume test of the new and improved Godzilla for a new era.

Top: Godzilla's fearsome new design.

Left: The introduction of Orga.

Overleaf: Godzilla and Orga face off in an epic final battle.

ゴジラ × メガギラス G消滅作戦

GODZILLA VS. MEGAGUIRUS (2000)

DIRECTOR : MASAAKI TEZUKA
WRITTEN BY : HIROSHI KASHIWABARA, WATARU MIMURA
PRODUCED BY : SHOGO TOMIYAMA
SPECIAL EFFECTS DIRECTOR : KENJI SUZUKI
SCORE : MICHIRU OSHIMA
STARRING : MISATO TANAKA, SHOSUKE TANIHARA, MASATO IBU, YURIKO HOSHI, TOSHIYUKI NAGASHIMA, TSUTOMU KITAGAWA, MINORU WATANABE

AS WOULD BE THE CASE WITH MOST OF THE FILMS IN THE MILLENNIUM ERA, GODZILLA'S NEXT ADVENTURE IGNORES THE EVENTS OF THE PREVIOUS FILMS (WITH THE EXCEPTION OF THE 1954 ORIGINAL) AND STANDS AS PART OF ITS OWN CONTINUITY.

Godzilla vs. Megaguirus opens with a recap of the events of Honda's 1954 original classic, told in black and white and superimposing the current incarnation of Godzilla over the familiar scenes of Tokyo's destruction in the original film. The ending is changed, however, and we are told that the Oxygen Destroyer did not kill Godzilla – in fact, Godzilla continued to torment Japan for years, attempting to siphon energy from Japan's many nuclear reactors.

As a result, nuclear energy was outlawed in the country, and for a time the people of Japan thrived following the discovery of a newer, cleaner form of energy: plasma. That too, unfortunately, proved to be an irresistible energy source for Godzilla, prompting the government to outlaw plasma as well. For a time, this strategy has worked, as Godzilla has remained slumbering beneath the ocean waves, with nothing calling it to Japan to resume its rampage.

In the intervening years, an experimental satellite has been launched into orbit. Dubbed the Dimension Tide, this satellite has the unique ability to create miniature black holes, and during a test of its capabilities opens a wormhole in space! A mysterious entity flies through the wormhole from whatever part of the universe (or different dimension) it originated and deposits a single egg before returning to its home. That egg falls to Earth, and of course finds its way to Japan.

A little boy finds the egg and brings it home, but is horrified when it begins to ooze and pulsate strangely. He tosses it into the sewer, where the egg hatches, and tiny dragonfly-like creatures emerge. These creatures begin to mutate and grow, and soon feed off the people of Osaka.

Eventually, Godzilla emerges from the sea in search of an apparent new source of nuclear energy (despite the country having not used any for decades) and is battled not only by the human-led G-Graspers (an elite anti-Godzilla military squad), but a swarm of hundreds of the tiny dragonfly creatures (dubbed Meganulas)!

The G-Graspers attempt to use the Dimension Tide to fire a black hole into Godzilla, but the attempt fails and it survives. Moreover, the surviving Meganulas have fed off of Godzilla's energy and have mutated into a full-grown Megaguirus! She is an enormous demonic dragonfly, capable of incredible speed and with a giant barbed stinger on her tail.

Godzilla and Megaguirus do epic battle, all while the humans attempt to use Dimension Tide once more to suck Godzilla into a black hole and rid the earth of it forever. With one final daring act by one of the G-Grasper pilots (a female hot shot major by the name of Kiriko Tsujimori, played with fire and heart by Misato Tanaka), the film culminates in an explosive finale that sees one of the most powerful creations in the cosmos come face to face with Earth's most fearsome monster.

The monster Megaguirus would be familiar to longtime Toho fans, as the creature was an evolution of the monster Meganulon, which first appeared in the film *Rodan* in 1956. This updating of the past, filled with reverence for the films that came before, was a hallmark of the Millennium Era, and *Godzilla vs. Megaguirus* was no different. This film also leans heavily into the horror aspects of the Godzilla franchise, with an adult aesthetic. It has a bouncy adventurous tone meshed with dark moments of terror as innocent people are abducted from the street by the growing Meganulas.

The franchise would lean even more heavily into its horror roots with its next instalment, while also bringing back a number of Godzilla's most famous foes. Yet again it would reset the timeline, and would also bring in a director who had, until this point, headlined one of Godzilla's biggest rival kaiju franchises...

ゴジラが消える。

超翔竜メガギラス、三段進化！
ブラックホール砲、炸裂!!
地球最大の死闘

12月16日(土)全国東宝系公開

ゴジラ×メガギラス
G消滅作戦

田中美里　谷原章介　伊武雅刀　星由里子
勝村政信　池内万作　山口馬木也　山下徹大／永島敏行　かとうかずこ　中村嘉葎雄
製作／富山省吾　脚本／柏原寛司・三村 渉　音楽／大島ミチル　GODZILLAテーマ曲／伊福部 昭　特殊技術／鈴木健二　監督／手塚昌明

製作／東宝映画　配給／東宝

© 2000 TOHO・TOHOEIGA

www.godzilla.co.jp

Opposite (above): Megaguirus in its final form.

Opposite (below): Megaguirus descends from the sky.

Above: Godzilla has a few new tricks for dealing with winged foes.

ゴジラ・モスラ・キングギドラ 大怪獣総攻撃

GODZILLA, MOTHRA AND KING GHIDORAH: GIANT MONSTERS ALL-OUT ATTACK (2001)

DIRECTOR : SHUSUKE KANEKO
WRITTEN BY : SHUSUKE KANEKO, KEIICHI HASEGAWA, MASAHIRO YOKOTANI
PRODUCED BY : HIDEYUKI HONMA
SPECIAL EFFECTS DIRECTOR : MAKOTO KAMIYA
SCORE : KOW OTANI
STARRING : CHIHARU NIIYAMA, RYUDO UZAKI, MASAHIRO KOBAYASHI, SHIRO SANO, TAKASHI NISHINA, MIZUHO YOSHIDA, AKIRA OHASHI, RIE OTA

FOR GODZILLA'S NEXT CHALLENGE, TOHO WOULD BRING ON BOARD A DIRECTOR WHO HAD HELMED A NUMBER OF MOVIES IN ONE OF THEIR BIGGEST RIVAL FRANCHISES: GAMERA.

Shusuke Kaneko had found great success directing the Gamera franchise throughout the 1990s, and would bring a fresh lens through which to view not only Godzilla the character but the spirit of the franchise as a whole.

Once more ignoring all of the previous entries from the franchise except for the 1954 original, *Godzilla, Mothra and King Ghidorah: Giant Monsters All-Out Attack* (which we'll shorten to simply *GMK*) begins in 2004, with the memory of the events of Godzilla's 1954 rampage weighing heavily on the world. Despite constant reminders of the importance of respect for history, and for the memory of those who died, people act with disrespect and cruelty, toppling ancient statues and forgetting the sacrifices made by those who came before.

Soon, Godzilla appears to be stirring in the ocean's depths. But how is that possible? It was destroyed by the Oxygen Destroyer 50 years prior! A young reporter is determined to find out, and throughout her investigation encounters an old man who appears to know quite a bit about what is going on.

Godzilla, it would seem, is a manifestation of the anger of all those who died in the Pacific Theater during the Second World War at the hands of the Imperial Japanese Army. The fact that present-day culture has forgotten them and their sacrifice has angered their spirits and they have resurrected Godzilla to remind the world of humility.

When Godzilla finally appears on land, it is truly an horrific sight. The most purely terrifying of any incarnation to date, it notably is missing pupils, with eyes pure white and soulless, full of vengeful malice.

Soon, three Guardian Monsters appear to protect the people from this evil Godzilla: Baragon, Mothra, and in a turn from its usual role as villain, King Ghidorah. Godzilla mercilessly destroys Baragon, and while Mothra and King Ghidorah certainly prove to be a challenge for Godzilla, it is down to a brave military general to face off the giant monster one-on-one in a desperate bid for ultimate survival.

GMK is perhaps the most pure horror film of the entire franchise, after the 1954 original. Ghostly visions, the snarling, sinister design of the new Godzilla, and the fact that it is paced like a slasher film make it truly scary. The spiritual angle that director Kaneko adds also gives a new poignancy to the idea behind the franchise: here, instead of an explicit nuclear fear, we are invited to respect the fear held by those of the previous generation. We may have forgotten what it was like to fear such things now in the new millennium, but the minute we forget – or worse, willfully ignore – those elements of our past, the past will return to haunt us. Further, the idea that the angry dead were those who died at the hands of the Japanese Army (as opposed to, for instance, the Americans or the Germans) is a pacifist indictment of wartime attrocities.

The film received near universal critical acclaim, and is commonly rated among the very best of the franchise. It manages to weave together the giant monster brawls that audiences crave, with meaningful commentary rooted in everything Ishiro Honda's original stood for. It frames Godzilla again as destroyer but more importantly as nature's checks and balances on humanity. When we get out of line, Godzilla is there to set us back on the proper path. By the end of this film, not only is the world safe from Godzilla once more but

生き残るのは誰だ!

ゴジラ モスラ キングギドラ

大怪獣総攻撃

破壊神ゴジラ日本上陸。
その時、天の神、海の神、地の神が
立ちあがった。

監督 金子修介

新山千春 宇崎竜童

www.godzilla.co.jp

through the trauma we have grown as a people. Daughters are even reunited with their fathers, with newfound mutual respect borne of the destruction and chaos. As a metaphor for when mankind comes together following a tragedy, it rarely gets more powerful and specific than that. Especially since this film was released a mere three months following the tragedy of September 11th, 2001, its reverence for the dead and insistence on honoring their memory through peace feels particularly relevant and powerful.

And that is why Godzilla has endured as long as it has: it functions as pure metaphor to shine a light on our greatest sins and our greatest triumphs.

The franchise would again reboot itself the following year with its next installment, a film that would bring the Millennium Era's signature style to one of Godzilla's most familiar and unflappable foes...

Opposite: Godzilla's new terrifying design, lacking pupils to give it a ghostly, vengeful presence.

Above: Mothra attempting to help humanity by battling the wrathful Godzilla.

Left: Chiharu Niiyama as Yuri Tachibana.

Above: King Ghidorah here as a guardian of the earth.

Left: Mothra yet again as a protector of humanity.

Opposite (above): The gruesome final battle.

Opposite (below): Yuri Tachibana, Teruaki Takeda (Masahiro Kobayashi), and Yutaka Hirose (Hiroyuki Watanabe).

Left: The vengeance spirit Godzilla wreaks havoc on Tokyo.

Above (top): Godzilla raised from the dead.

Above Middle: Baragon crests a hill.

Above: Godzilla, deadlier and more horrifying than ever before.

Opposite (above): Godzilla versus two of Earth's guardians.

Opposite (below): Baragon arriving to protect Earths.

Above: Godzilla ready for battle.

Left: Godzilla about to unleash its devastating heat ray.

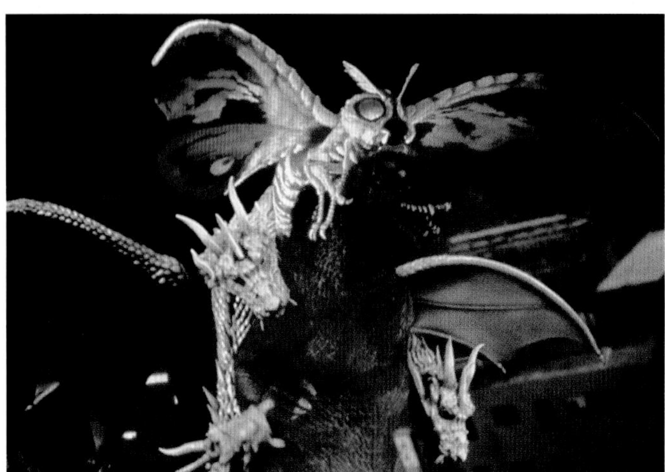

Above (top): King Ghidorah, golden and deadly.

Above (middle): Mothra descending upon Godzilla.

Above: Mothra and King Ghidorah team up against the evil Godzilla.

Right: King Ghidorah raining destruction from the skies.

ゴジラ×メカゴジラ

GODZILLA AGAINST MECHAGODZILLA (2002)

DIRECTOR : MASAAKI TEZUKA
WRITTEN BY : WATARU MIMURA
PRODUCED BY : SHOGO TOMIYAMA
SPECIAL EFFECTS DIRECTOR : YUICHI KIKUCHI
SCORE : MICHIRU OSHIMA
STARRING : YUMIKO SHAKU, SHIN TAKUMA, KANA ONODERA, KO TAKASUGI, YUSUKE TOMOI, TSUTOMU KITAGAWA, HIROFUMI ISHIGAKI

FOLLOWING IN THE TRADITION OF THE MILLENNIUM FILMS THAT CAME BEFORE IT, *GODZILLA AGAINST MECHAGODZILLA* RESETS THE TIMELINE ONCE MORE, IGNORING ALL PREVIOUS ENTRIES EXCEPT FOR THE 1954 ORIGINAL.

This new film would again focus on the grim horrors of memories past, but this time through the lens of a group of hardened ace pilots and technology too powerful for even them to control.

It's the year 1999, and Godzilla has returned to destroy Tokyo. In a harrowing opening scene, Lieutenant Akane Yashiro is operating a powerful Maser Cannon and attempts to use the deadly weapon to kill the rampaging Godzilla. She fails, and inadvertently causes the deaths of several fellow soldiers in a neighboring vehicle.

Following the tragedy, she is demoted and shunned by her peers. Meanwhile, a new Godzilla-killing project is unveiled: a gigantic cyborg in the form of Godzilla that has been implanted with the bones of the long-dead original Godzilla! With a combination of modern technology and the DNA of the very beast they wish to destroy, this new Mechagodzilla (codename Kiryu) will spell the end of the monster when it returns once again. And who will pilot this incredible new weapon? Disgraced former Maser Cannon technician Akane Yashiro.

The film follows Akane through her training, as well as her struggles within the pilot community as many still blame her for the deaths of their compatriots. Many don't trust her abilities, and challenges to her capability in piloting this machine come daily. The tone reminds us of films like *Top Gun*, a microscopic view of the inner world and social complexities of elite fighters that in these films are normally relegated to miniatures flying past a giant monster only to get destroyed. Here, we see inside the cockpit.

Fast-forward four years, and Godzilla does eventually attack again. Kiryu is dispatched for its inaugural fight, with Akane at the helm, and the battle is fierce and brimming with incredible power on both sides. Kiryu, it seems, may in fact actually be a Godzilla killer.

During the battle, however, the unexpected occurs when Godzilla unleashes its signature roar. The giant cyborg hears this roar, and the bones inside trigger a flood of memories from the original 1954 rampage and it suddenly begins acting of its own accord! Kiryu turns on the city, launching into a terrifying storm of destruction throughout the city as Akane helplessly watches on in horror. Godzilla retreats, and Kiryu's rampage doesn't end until it runs out of power.

Of course her fellow pilots blame Akane, her first time out with this powerful new weapon resulting yet again in death and destruction while she claims to have been helpless. The mecha is repaired and ready when Godzilla attacks again, and Akane must now prove both to herself and her squad mates that she is capable of defending the city. In this gargantuan final battle of the film, she does indeed prove herself, and after a fight filled with twists, turns, and some truly daring life-threatening heroics by Akane, Godzilla is sent limping back out to sea.

Godzilla Against Mechagodzilla was an enormous box office success, the biggest money-maker of the Millennium Era. Audiences responded to the complex plot following disgraced pilot Akane, and her personal turmoil in trying to be accepted by her comrades as well as forgive herself for the opening scene's tragic mistake.

In a franchise where the military is often depicted merely as miniatures firing ineffective missiles at towering monsters on a rampage, *Godzilla Against Mechagodzilla* gives us a new respect for the people inside those tiny tanks. It gives perspective on their human sacrifice, and even the emotional impact of bearing witness to the horrors of a kaiju attack. By placing a magnifying glass over what would in most other films be an ineffectual blip in the action (the destruction of a tank beneath Godzilla's foot), the film retroactively lends more weight to all the films that came before it.

The next year, director Masaaki Tezuka would return with a direct sequel to this film, breaking from the previous Millennium mold – in more ways than one. He would expand the world of this tech-heavy military story to include magic, mysticism, and a very familiar friend of humanity...

起動・共鳴・氷砕

ゴジラ×メカゴジラ

砕け散るまで戦え！

監督◇手塚昌明　釈由美子　宅麻 伸　高杉 亘　友井雄亮　水野久美　中尾 彬

製作◇富山省吾　エグゼクティブプロデューサー◇森知貴秀　脚本◇三村 渉　音楽◇大島ミチル　特殊技術◇菊地雄一

撮影◇岸本正広　美術◇瀬下幸治　録音◇斉藤禎一　照明◇望月英樹　編集◇[illegible]　キャスティング◇田中忠雄　助監督◇[illegible]　製作担当者◇金澤清美　音響効果◇佐々木英世

（特殊技術）撮影◇江口憲一　特美◇三池敏夫　照明◇斉藤 薫　造形◇若狭新一　特効◇[illegible]　助監督◇野間詳令　製作担当者◇川田尚広　（視覚効果）プロデュース◇小川利弘　協力◇防衛庁

製作◇東宝映画　配給◇東宝

Above: Mechagodzilla being hoisted into the studio rafters by wires.

Left: Behind the scenes photo of Mechagodzilla before a painted backdrop.

Opposite: A new and improved Mechagodzilla design.

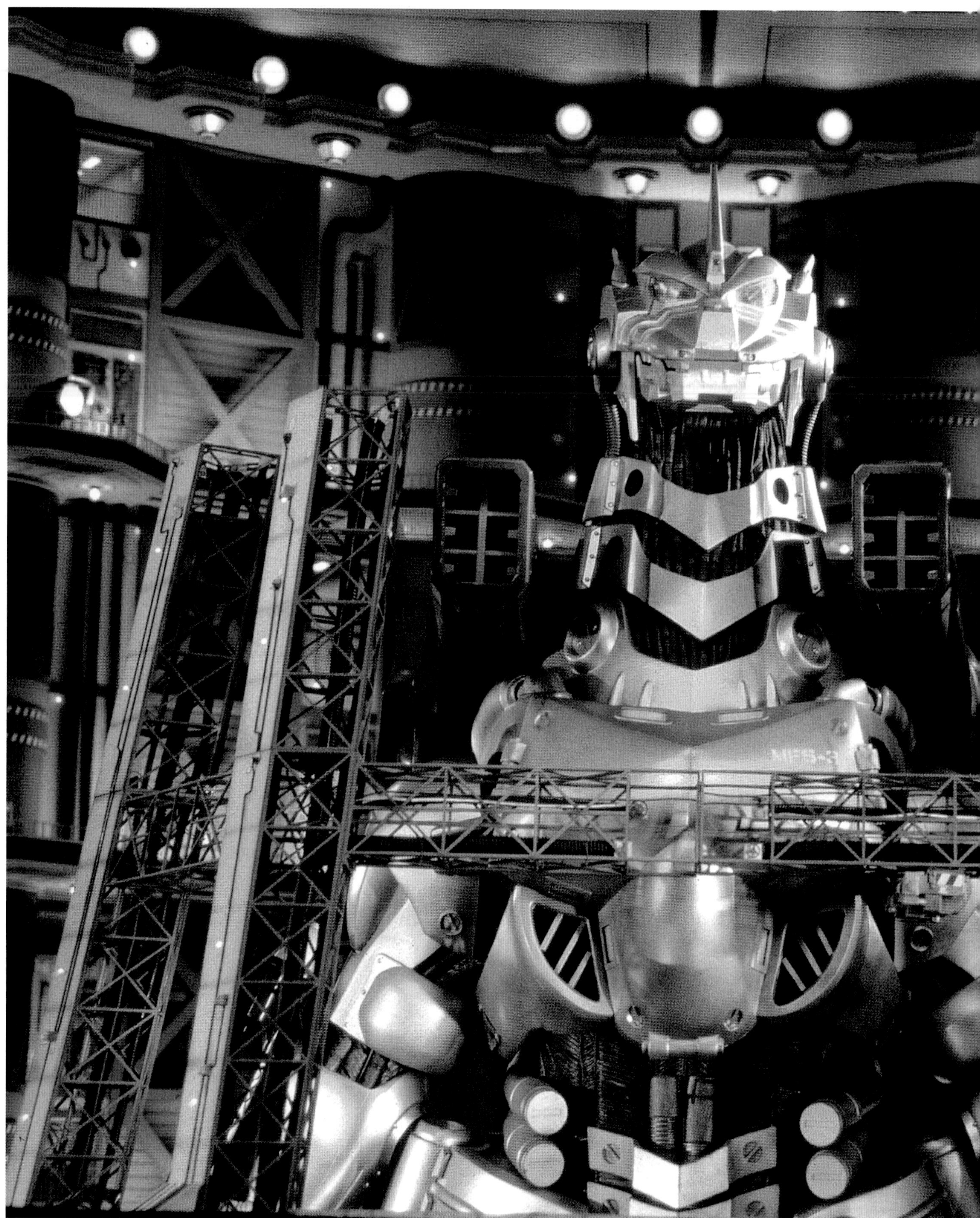
MFS-3

Left: Mechagodzilla preparing for launch.

Above (top): Mechagodzilla's final form.

Above: Mechagodzilla finally vanguished.

ゴジラ×モスラ×メカゴジラ 東京SOS

GODZILLA: TOKYO S.O.S. (2003)

DIRECTOR : MASAAKI TEZUKA
WRITTEN BY : MASAAKI TEZUKA, MASAHIRO YOKOTANI
PRODUCED BY : SHOGO TOMIYAMA
SPECIAL EFFECTS DIRECTOR : EIICHI ASADA
SCORE : MICHIRU OSHIMA
STARRING : NOBORU KANEKO, MIHO YOSHIOKA, MICKEY KOGA, HIROSHI KOIZUMI, AKIRA NAKAO, TSUTOMU KITAGAWA, MOTOKUNI NAKAGAWA

IN THIS IMMEDIATE FOLLOW-UP TO *GODZILLA AGAINST MECHAGODZILLA*, SCIENTISTS HAVE BEEN WORKING FOR A YEAR TO REPAIR KIRYU AFTER ITS DEVASTATING FINAL BATTLE WITH GODZILLA FROM THE PREVIOUS FILM.

Surprisingly, the prime minister then receives an unexpected pair of guests: the Shobijin from Infant Island! The magical tiny twin fairies who commune with Mothra arrive to tell him that the reason Godzilla keeps attacking is because they have taken its bones from the ocean for use in Kiryu. If they return the bones to the ocean, Godzilla will once more be at peace and will no longer attack. Of course, this means that the entire Kiryu project will have to be scrapped, which would leave Japan defenseless in case the fairies are incorrect.

They tell him that Mothra will step in to protect Japan if need be, but – again breaking tradition with the previous Millennium films – the prime minister notes that Mothra attacked Japan during the events of 1961's *Mothra* and therefore doesn't trust the giant moth goddess.

Actor Hiroshi Koizumi – best known in this franchise for his starring role in *Godzilla Raids Again*, returns here to reprise his role as Dr. Shinichi Chujo from Honda's original film *Mothra*, attempting to convince the prime minister that the only reason Mothra attacked Japan in the first place was because the Shobijin had been stolen from their home, and she was coming to save them. It had been man's fault for bringing the monster to our shores, just as it is now.

Still, the hubris of man is difficult to dispel, and the prime minister will not agree. Man will kill Godzilla, and Kiryu will be the weapon to do it.

Eventually, Godzilla, Kiryu, Mothra, and two newly-hatched Mothra larvae (one of which is the first appearance of a male Mothra so far in all of the films) all meet in battle in Tokyo and mayhem ensues. At a certain point, young scientist Yoshito Chujo – the son of Koizumi's Shinichi Chujo – must perform a daring tech surgery on Kiryu during battle when the mecha gets disabled. He becomes trapped inside of Kiryu as the battle comes to a cacophonous finale. There is the familiar – but always tragic – self-sacrifice by protector Mothra. A moving moment comes when we learn that the spirit of the original Godzilla within Kiryu's body recognizes and appreciates the work that scientist Chujo has done to bring it to life.

Eventually, Kiryu once again takes control of its own body, carrying Godzilla (who was destined for destruction by Kiryu's powerful secret weapon) out to sea, where it plummets both he and Godzilla down to the ocean floor. The bones have been returned, and Godzilla can finally slumber in peace.

Continuing the theme of the power of memory from the previous film, *Godzilla: Tokyo S.O.S.* also focuses on the need for mankind to accept responsibility for its actions, a message strikingly similar to Honda's 1954 original film. Yes, Mothra did attack Tokyo once upon a time, but only because we had stolen that which was precious to her. Additionally, themes of forgiveness flow through this film, as although Godzilla had attacked Tokyo in 1954, pure revenge (which the prime minister seems to desire) is not the answer. We have effectively awoken Godzilla by removing its bones from their resting place in order to simply destroy it once more. It's a vicious cycle, and only by putting our weapons down will the cycle finally end.

This film has a more family-oriented tone than the previous movie, and audiences of all ages responded well to the return of the mystical Mothra and her fairies from Infant Island. Toho would use this momentum to create one final film of the Millennium Era the following year, a year that also happened to coincide with the 50th anniversary of the release of Honda's original. It would be bigger, louder, and more explosive than any Godzilla film to date, a fitting way to send off the Millennium Era in style and pay raucous homage to the King on its 50th birthday...

大怪獣頂上決戦

ゴジラ×モスラ×メカゴジラ

東京SOS

お願いです！ゴジラの骨を海に返してください

金子 昇　吉岡美穂　虎牙光揮　長澤まさみ・大塚ちひろ　高杉 亘　小泉 博　中尾 彬

監督■手塚昌明　製作■富山省吾　脚本■横谷昌宏・手塚昌明　音楽■大島ミチル　特殊技術■浅田英一

www.godzilla.co.jp

12.13（土）東宝系公開

Above (top): Kamoebas miniature.

Above: Mothra suspended from the Toho Sound Stage rafters.

Right: Mechagodzilla preparing to fire its ultimate weapon.

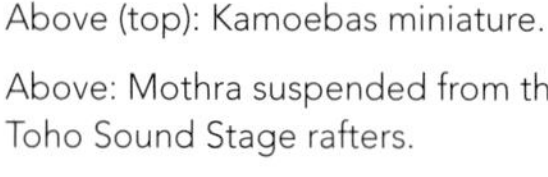

MFS-3

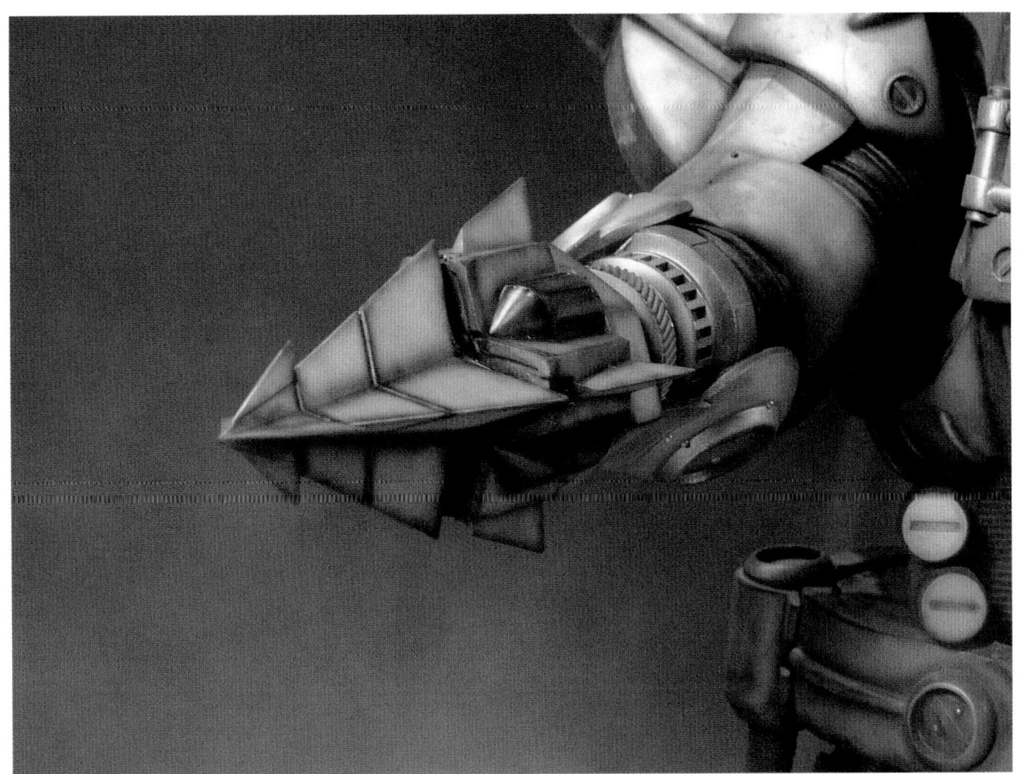

Opposite: Mechagodzilla's newest incarnation, bulkier and more intimidating than ever.

Top: Mechagodzilla's formidable drill attachment.

Above: A model of the Tokyo Tower is illuminated on the *Tokyo S.O.S.* set.

Top: The Mothra larvae crawl through the city ruins.

Above: Godzilla and Mechagodzilla in their final battle.

Opposite: Mechagodzilla's intimidating final form.

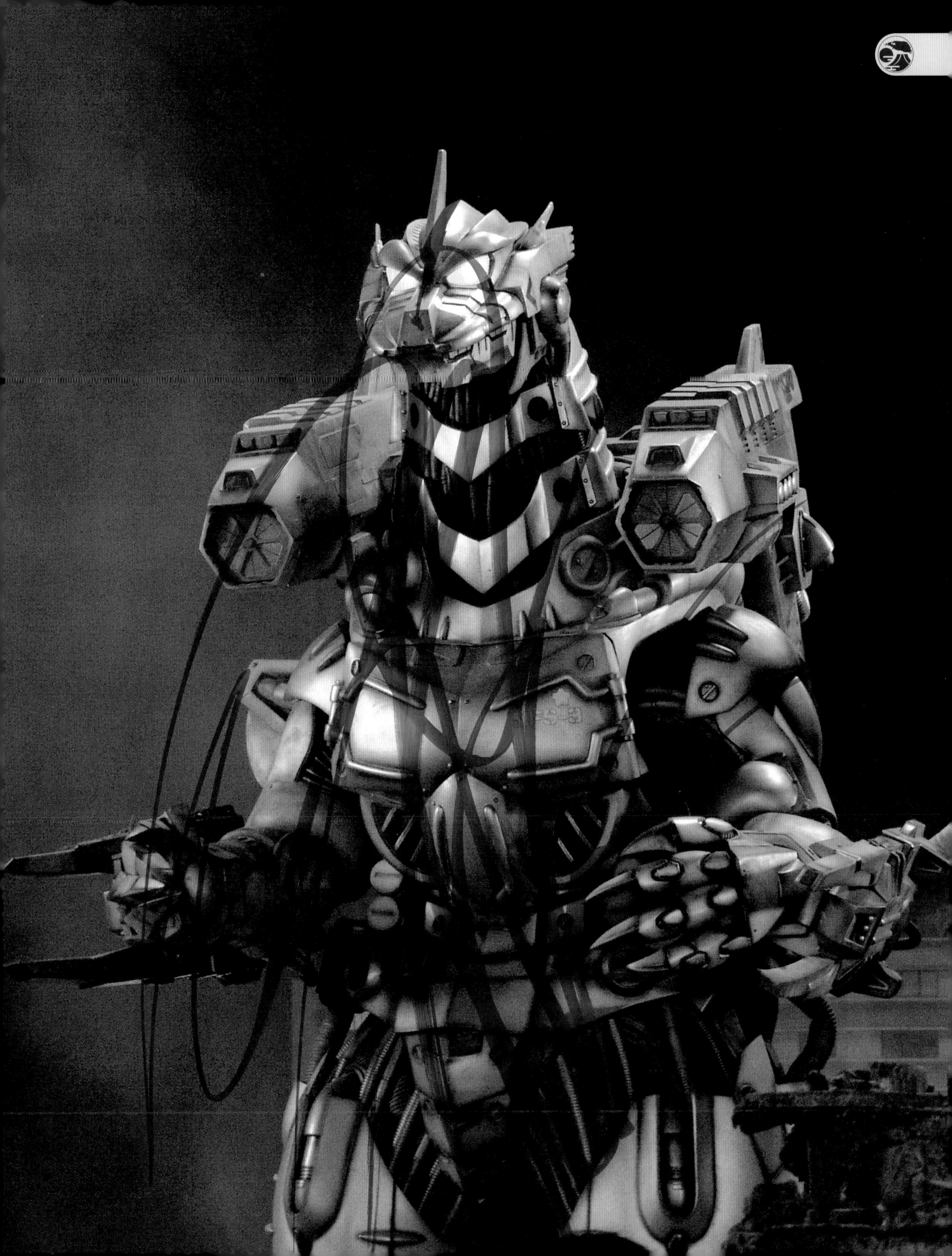

ゴジラ ファイナル ウォーズ

GODZILLA: FINAL WARS (2004)

DIRECTOR : RYUHEI KITAMURA
WRITTEN BY : RYUHEI KITAMURA, ISAO KIRIYAMA
PRODUCED BY : SHOGO TOMIYAMA
SPECIAL EFFECTS DIRECTOR : EIICHI ASADA
SCORE : KEITH EMERSON, NOBUHIKO MORINO, DAISUKE YANO
STARRING : MASAHIRO MATSUOKA, REI KIKUKAWA, DON FRYE, MAKI MIZUNO, AKIRA TAKARADA, KAZUKI KITAMURA, KUMI MIZUNO, KENJI SAHARA, TSUTOMU KITAGAWA, NAOKO KAMIO, KAZUHIRO YOSHIDA, TOSHIHIRO OGURA, MOTOKUNI NAKAGAWA

FOR GODZILLA'S 50TH ANNIVERSARY, TOHO WENT TO FAMED HORROR/SCI-FI/ACTION DIRECTOR RYUHEI KITAMURA TO DELIVER A NO-HOLDS-BARRED EXPLOSIVE SPECTACLE THAT WOULD CELEBRATE THE WORLD'S FAVORITE KAIJU'S 50-YEAR HISTORY IN AN UNFORGETTABLE WAY.

Kitamura produced a true love letter to the series, especially the Showa Era, with a high fantasy sci-fi human plot, appearances from nearly every monster from the entire franchise, and lots of bombastic monster-on-monster action. If this was to be the Final War, it would go out with style.

The film opens by yet again resetting the continuity of the series, with Godzilla being trapped in ice in Antarctica after a battle with the *Gotengo* – a classic battleship featuring a massive drill that first appeared in the Toho film *Atragon*, a 1963 classic directed by Godzilla creator Ishiro Honda. Here, the *Gotengo* is captained by American human tank Captain Gordon, played with steely swagger by MMA superstar Don Frye.

In the ensuing years, however, monsters around the world continue to threaten mankind as a result of climate change and pollution, as well as the lack of Godzilla as counterbalance to the villainous kaiju.

Meanwhile, Earth has assembled a team of elite soldiers known as M-Force, a squadron of mutant warriors imbued with a strange strand of DNA that makes them super-fast, super-strong, and with telekinetic abilities. In Godzilla's absence, they are Earth's best defense against whatever monsters may arise.

Scientists discover that these mutants share DNA with only one other creature on Earth: a huge mummified ancient kaiju known as Gigan, who had battled Mothra thousands of years ago. The Shobijin arrive to warn the scientists that a war is coming, a final war between good and evil, and that the mutant Ozaki – the most powerful mutant soldier in M-Force – would face a crisis that would determine whether he himself was on the side of good, or would help in destroying humanity.

Suddenly, kaiju around the world erupt from the earth and begin attacking cities. Rodan is in New York City, King Caesar in Okinawa and Anguirus returns in Shanghai. Kamacuras appears as well, as does Kumonga, Ebirah, Hedorah, and even the all-CGI version of the American Roland Emmerich's Godzilla (here simply called Zilla) in Sydney. Even Minilla returns, befriending a young boy in the forest and embarking on an adorable road trip to find his monstrous father.

The monsters wreak utter havoc around the globe, leaving humanity totally defenseless against the slaughter. Fortunately, a group of UFOs appear seemingly out of nowhere and are able to instantaneously zap all of the monsters out of existence! With the world quiet once more, the UFO lands and its inhabitants – the aliens known as the Xiliens – introduce themselves to the human race, declaring their intent to be friends to mankind.

The new secretary of the UN – played by original Godzilla actor Akira Takarada – declares that Earth will join with the Xiliens and become a part of a new galactic civilization. Some aren't quite so convinced, however, and a sinister plot is unveiled that the Xiliens are not as friendly as they seem. This of course will be no surprise to fans of the Godzilla franchise, but it turns out the Xiliens have replaced several high-ranking members of the world government, including the UN Secretary General.

A battle ensues between the remaining members of M-Force and the equally powerful Xiliens. Gigan is resurrected by the aliens, and mankind knows the only solution is to resurrect Earth's greatest warrior: Godzilla.

Massive monster battles explode around the world, with Godzilla destroying each kaiju one by one, working its way to Tokyo to challenge the UFO itself. At the same time, M-Force battles the Xiliens in a number of increasingly wild showdowns, notably a lengthy motorcycle chase with acrobatic martial arts as they speed down a deserted highway.

This super-charged film results in a final battle befitting the King of the Monsters, with Gigan, Mothra, and even King Ghidorah facing off against Godzilla in a ruined Tokyo. The climax is steeped in deep

さらば、ゴジラ。
２０XX年。世界中で出現した怪獣に対し、
地球防衛軍は人類の存亡をかけて ファイナル・ウォーズに挑む。
その頃、ゴジラは南極の氷の中で眠り続けていた・・・
シリーズ50年の集大成 最高峰にして最終作
GODZILLA
FINAL WARS
ゴジラ ファイナル ウォーズ
監督■北村龍平 主演■松岡昌宏 菊川 怜
製作■富山省吾 脚本■三村 渉・桐山 勲 特殊技術■浅田英一 製作◆東宝映画 配給◆東宝
2004年12月4日(土)全国東宝系拡大ロードショー
50th
1954-2004

"THERE IS SOMETHING TRULY POETIC IN KITAMURA'S APPROACH AS CELEBRATION OF THE FRANCHISE, OF GIVING AUDIENCES THE SAME JOY OF WATCHING THESE ICONIC MONSTERS BATTLE WHILE UPDATING THE EFFECTS AND ACTION WITH A MODERN SENSIBILITY."

love for Godzilla not only as a character but also the franchise as a whole, bursting with reverence and a childlike destructive glee.

Director Kitamura stated that he wanted his film to harken back to the raucous fun of the Showa Era, and that veneration shines throughout the film. Music legend Keith Emerson was brought onboard by Kitamura to score the film, adding a layer of synth-rock electricity to the eruptive proceedings.

Godzilla: Final Wars serves as an appropriate culmination of not only the Millennium Era, but also the 50-year trilogy of Eras that began with the original film. There is something truly poetic in Kitamura's approach as celebration of the franchise, of giving audiences the same joy of watching these iconic monsters battle while updating the effects and action with a modern sensibility. Kitamura was careful to keep his monsters practical, with actors in suits, as opposed to a more conventional modern approach of relying on CGI, as a way of not only retaining the tactile feel of the Showa Era, but also the concussive impact that only comes with two actors actually slamming each other into the ground. (One monster would be CGI, the "tuna-eating" Zilla, as a not-so-subtle dig at Hollywood's penchant for making all of their monsters computer generated as opposed to actual humans in suits.)

The film was a huge success, ending the Millennium Era on a high note, and leaving fans the world over curious if Godzilla would ever re-emerge from his home studio. Would this actually mark the end of Godzilla's reign as the King of the Monsters?

A full decade would pass before Godzilla would awaken once again, this time not in Japan, but as a menace to an unsuspecting America...

Right: The mysterious Monster X in the final battle across a ruined Tokyo.

Above: Gigan's resurrection is the spark that sets off *Final Wars*.

Left: Hedorah and Ebirah collide.

Opposite (above): Godzilla in Antarctica.

Opposite (right): Manda wrapping itself around the *Gotengo*.

Left: The all-new Keizer Ghidorah pummels Godzilla.

Top: The all-CGI tuna-eating Zilla, a meta play on Roland Emmerich's recent American reimagining.

Above: Kitamura's personal favorite monster, King Caesar, here to do battle once more.

ゴジラ

令和

THE REIWA ERA

In 2016 Toho Studios ushered Godzilla into its current era with *Shin Godzilla*, and set the stage for a bright and bold future for the mythic monster. With new films on the horizon, as well as a trilogy of animated features and the animated series *Godzilla Singular Point*, Toho establishes with its newest era that it is continuing to take Godzilla in brave and uncharted directions. If the quality and success of its award-winning debut feature is any indication, the Reiwa Era of Godzilla may turn out to be its most daring yet...

THE REIWA ERA FILMS ARE:

2016 SHIN GODZILLA

2017 GODZILLA: PLANET OF THE MONSTERS

2018 GODZILLA: CITY ON THE EDGE OF BATTLE

2019 GODZILLA: THE PLANET EATER

シン・ゴジラ

SHIN GODZILLA (2016)

DIRECTOR : HIDEAKI ANNO, SHINJI HIGUCHI
WRITTEN BY : HIDEAKI ANNO
SPECIAL EFFECTS PRODUCTION DESIGNER : TOSHIO MIIKE
SCORE : SHIRO SAGISU
STARRING : HIROKI HASEGAWA, SATOMI ISHIHARA, REN OSUGI, MANSAI NOMURA

SHORTLY AFTER THE SUCCESS OF LEGENDARY PICTURES' AMERICAN REBOOT OF GODZILLA IN 2014, TOHO SET INTO MOTION A NEW JAPANESE GODZILLA THAT WOULD SERVE AS A RESET OF THE FRANCHISE FROM THE STUDIO THAT STARTED IT ALL.

Bringing on esteemed directors Hideaki Anno and Shinji Higuchi, who had both created the seminal anime TV series *Neon Genesis Evangelion*, this new *Godzilla* would not only mark the beginning of a new era for Japan's most popular cinematic creation, but would also mark the largest Godzilla to date!

Instead of standing in as an allegory for the atomic bomb, *Shin Godzilla* would serve as a symbol for the Fukushima Daiichi disaster that had happened just a few years previously. Like the original film, *Shin Godzilla* would use the presence of and attack by the monster to echo the devastation and terror of the 2011 earthquake and tsunami that resulted in such a tragedy. It would also allow for satirical commentary about the government's ineptitude in responding to such a crisis. Truly a concept that harkens back to the roots of what made Godzilla such an enduring symbol in the first place.

The story tells of a government caught off-guard, faced with some phenomena in Tokyo Bay that seems to indicate a giant creature, but which government officials are hesitant to label as anything other than "geothermal activity" for fear of public panic. Of course, the problem indeed proves itself to be a huge monster, one that lumbers onto land as a strange, evolving amphibian that destroys an entire neighborhood as it stumbles around.

While people die, the government bureaucrats fumble with their response: do they evacuate, and how quickly? Should the military respond? How will that look to the media? Should they kill this creature, or study it?

Eventually, the creature retreats to the sea when its body begins to overheat, only to return later in a new form: now walking upright, and looking much more familiar to audiences as the Godzilla that we fear and revere.

Every government response appears to only cause more death and destruction, with bombing runs and tank attacks only serving to enrage the monster further, or spark powerful counterattacks from the creature that send beams of pure energy blasting out in all directions.

Finally, a theory is agreed upon that would see the government attempt to freeze the monster, all in the looming shadow of yet another nuclear detonation on Japanese soil. The government's ability to respond to this threat would prove crucial in hopefully preventing Japan from yet again becoming the sole victim of the world's atomic legacy.

For *Shin Godzilla*, Toho succeeded in not only tapping into what made Honda's 1954 original so compelling, but also rebuilding Godzilla's legacy from the foundation, with a whole new (yet familiar) creature design, as well as establishing a new foundation on which to build the new era of Japan's most iconic monster.

Actor Mansai Nomura would inhabit Godzilla through motion capture. A decorated stage actor, Nomura brought his training in Kyogen (a classic Japanese form of comedic theatre) to the role, echoing original Godzilla actor Haruo Nakajima's commitment to treating Godzilla as a character, rather than simply a glorified prop. Nomura's Godzilla moves with a heavy-footed elegance that reminds us of the original monster. This new Godzilla is both contemplative and destructive – a true force of nature.

"FOR SHIN GODZILLA, TOHO SUCCEEDED IN NOT ONLY TAPPING INTO WHAT MADE HONDA'S 1954 ORIGINAL SO COMPELLING, BUT ALSO REBUILDING GODZILLA'S LEGACY FROM THE FOUNDATION, WITH A WHOLE NEW (YET FAMILIAR) CREATURE DESIGN."

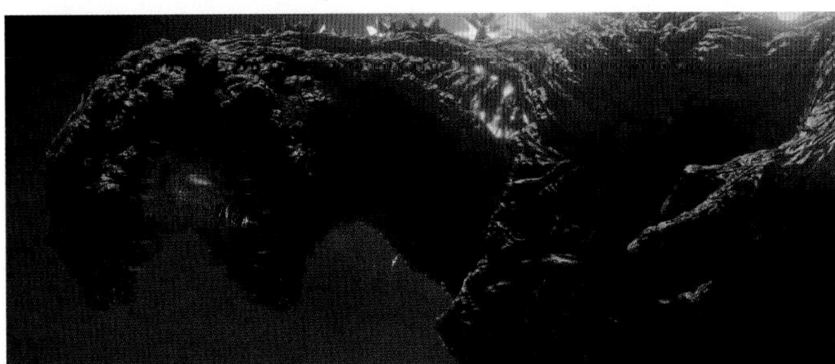

Shin Godzilla would go on to win Japan's highest cinematic honor: Picture of the Year at the Japan Academy Awards. Anno and Higuchi would also win for Best Director. Over 60 years after their most famous creation was born, Toho Studios reminded the world that they were, without a doubt, the masters of the monster. Not only could they bring back Godzilla as a terrifying force of sci-fi destruction, but they could do so with grace, emotion, and vital social commentary – the hallmarks of what made Honda's first film so lasting and important.

This film would launch the current era of the Godzilla franchise, and remind the world that while the King of the Monsters may take many forms (both literally and figuratively), its influence and impact on popular culture remain undeniable. Toho Studios birthed Godzilla into the world, and yet again they redefine it for a new era.

Shin Godzilla has many meanings: "New Godzilla", "True Godzilla", and even "God Godzilla". Regardless of what translation you adhere to, one thing is certain: Godzilla is eternal. Toho continues to let its beast grow and evolve, and its most recent films bring Godzilla into a whole new form yet again...

Top: The final form of Godzilla withstanding a hail of gunfire.

Above (top left): One of the various forms Godzilla takes in the film.

Above (middle left): Shin Godzilla preparing its all-new heat ray.

Left: The form Godzilla fans refer to as "Kamata-kun"

40

Opposite (top left): Godzilla undergoes a number of transformations.

Opposite (left middle): For the first time in the film, Godzilla lets out its classic roar.

Opposite (left bottom): CGI rendering of Godzilla.

Above: Despite assurances that it would not, Godzilla makes landfall.

Left: Godzilla's formidable claws now fully grown.

GODZILLA: PLANET OF THE MONSTERS (2017)

DIRECTOR : HIROYUKI SESHITA, KOBUN SHIZUNO
WRITTEN BY : GEN UROBUCHI
PRODUCED BY : TAKASHI YOSHIZAWA
SCORE : TAKAYUKI HATTORI
STARRING : MAMORU MIYANO, TAKAHIRO SAKURAI, KANA HANAZAWA, TOMOKAZU SUGITA, YUKI KAJI

AS *SHIN GODZILLA* WAS STOMPING AROUND THE WORLD IN ITS CRITICALLY ACCLAIMED RELEASE, TOHO STUDIOS ANNOUNCED A NEW ENDEAVOR TO BRING GODZILLA TO HOMES AROUND THE GLOBE: A TRILOGY OF ANIMATED GODZILLA FILMS THAT WOULD BE RELEASED EXCLUSIVELY ON STREAMING GIANT NETFLIX.

Popular anime directors Kobun Shizuno and Hiroyuki Seshita crafted a new chronology for the Godzilla universe, set in the distant future on an Earth no longer dominated by humans. In this world, Godzilla truly reigns supreme. It will fall to a group of humans struggling with identity, faith, and their relationship to technology to take the planet back from the King of the Monsters.

In the film, at the end of the 20th century, humanity was forced to evacuate Earth due to the kaiju taking over and decimating civilization. The chief of these is Godzilla, a gargantuan being that ultimately has won out over all of the other monsters and appears to be impervious to any attempts to harm it.

Two alien races, the Exif and the Bilusaludo, arrive on Earth to help rid the planet of Godzilla, but to no avail. It's also suspected that their motives may not be entirely altruistic. Eventually, the two extraterrestrial races and all of mankind are forced to flee, hoping to stake a claim on a new world only a few light years away.

When the first transport ship to their new planetary home is destroyed, the decision is made to return to Earth and retake what was once theirs. Upon landing, however, they learn that due to relativistic time dilation (after traveling at light speed for so long), 20,000 years have passed on Godzilla's Earth, whereas only 20 have elapsed for the humans. The world is a much different place than when they left it.

The humans, Exif and the Bilusaludo team up to attempt to disable Godzilla's electricity-producing dorsal spines, and then trap the beast beneath a mountain. The battle is hard fought, but ultimately the foe they believe to be Godzilla is proven to be merely an offspring of the real deal. The real Godzilla is awoken, towering over everything on the planet, and swiftly destroys any hope the humans have of reclaiming their planet.

An end credits scene sets up the next film, with our hero waking up to a mysterious native girl, having apparently been saved from the devastating blast...

The chronological blank slate at the start of this movie allows the filmmakers to tap into a number of truly unique ideas, and really ask key questions: Whose planet is this? Is it humanity's? Or are we simply a part of the food chain, deceived by centuries of perceived dominance?

Additionally, the Exif and the Bilusaludo are at two ends of the philosophical spectrum – the Exif views existence from a religious point of view, while the Bilusaludo is devoted (religiously) to technology and the pursuit of intellectual dominance. This asks further questions and forces the humans of the story to walk a line between the two. Such is life for mankind now, caught in a tug of war between spirituality and technology. That challenge is amplified in the world of *Planet of the Monsters*.

Development of the second and third entries in this trilogy was already underway when *Planet of the Monsters* was released, so audiences didn't have to wait long to discover what would become of Haruo and his ragtag battalion of humans and aliens seeking to destroy a seemingly immortal monster. In the next entry, however, the question of the limits of the power of technology would be brought to the forefront, and humanity must decide whether it's better to destroy nature with science, or to simply let Mother Earth do as she wishes...

Opposite (top left): The alien ship orbiting a future Earth.

Opposite (top right): Godzilla's devastating new version of its signature heat ray.

Opposite (middle left): The Bilusaludo ship console, mapping Godzilla's power.

Opposite (middle right): Godzilla ravages the world.

Opposite (below): Humans from the far future view an Earth very different from our own.

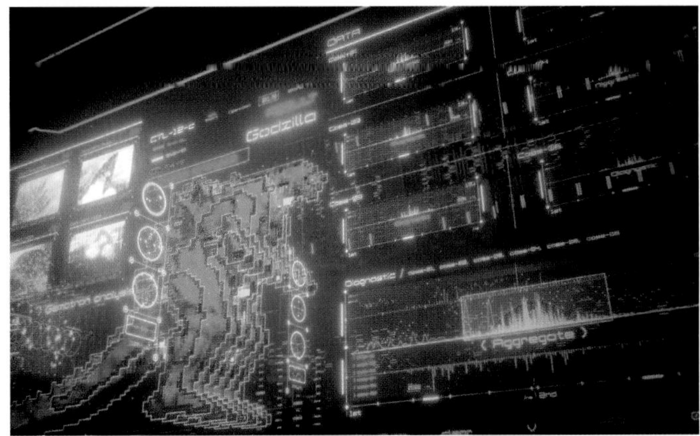
Godzilla
(Aggregate)

GODZILLA 決戦機動増殖都市

GODZILLA: CITY ON THE EDGE OF BATTLE (2018)

DIRECTOR : HIROYUKI SESHITA, KOBUN SHIZUNO
WRITTEN BY : GEN UROBUCHI, SADAYUKI MURAI, TETSUYA YAMADA
PRODUCED BY : TAKASHI YOSHIZAWA
SCORE : TAKAYUKI HATTORI
STARRING : MAMORU MIYANO, TAKAHIRO SAKURAI, KANA HANAZAWA, TOMOKAZU SUGITA, YUKI KAJI

FOLLOWING THE CATASTROPHE AT THE END OF THE PREVIOUS FILM, THE MOTHER SHIP IS PREPARED TO ABANDON THE TASK OF RETAKING EARTH AND LEAVE THE PLANET TO THE MONSTERS IF ANY SURVIVORS ARE UNABLE TO BE FOUND WITHIN THE NEXT TWO DAYS.

Meanwhile, our hero Haruo awakens in a hut under the care of not one, but two young twin women, surviving ancestors of humanity that are the trusted guardians of a giant egg, the final remnant of their long-lost deity.

It's discovered that the ladies' arrowheads are made of a precious nanometal, one that has only ever appeared at one point in history: the creation of Mechagodzilla. The nanometal's energy signature is traced back to the original construction facility – now more like its own city – where Mechagodzilla was built. Our heroes learn that over the ensuing 20,000 years, the nanoparticles have spread and evolved, consuming the entire city and forming a sentient mind of their own.

In an effort to use the existence of Mechagodzilla's nanometal to destroy Godzilla, the technology-worshipping Bilusaludo fuse with the city itself, sacrificing their individuality to become a hive mind that together can be powerful enough to destroy the King of the Monsters once and for all. Humanity must confront whether they want to give up their souls in order to win, or destroy the only thing capable of helping them conquer Godzilla once and for all. A daring final battle culminates in a tragic loss, as well as allies turning on one another as the titular City finally goes to war.

Godzilla 2000: Millennium composer Takayuki Hattori returned to create the score for the three films in this trilogy, creating a link between eras and bringing a classic Godzilla sensibility into a new animated age. Critics also praised the continuation of the story from the first film in the trilogy, as well as the expansion of the mythology. By the end, fans were clamoring to find out what the explosive conclusion to this trilogy would be, and were tantalized by the mention of a single name by one of the Exif mystics, the name of the monster that had destroyed their world, a monster even more powerful than Godzilla.

Its name was *Ghidorah*...

Top: Godzilla wreaks destruction on this future Earth.

Above: Godzilla's heat ray is more powerful than ever.

Opposite (above): The new iteration of the Shobijin, these young native women protect a giant mystical egg.

Opposite (below): The alien race has their sights set on destroying Godzilla once and for all.

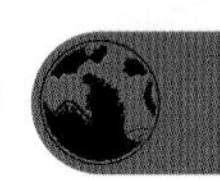

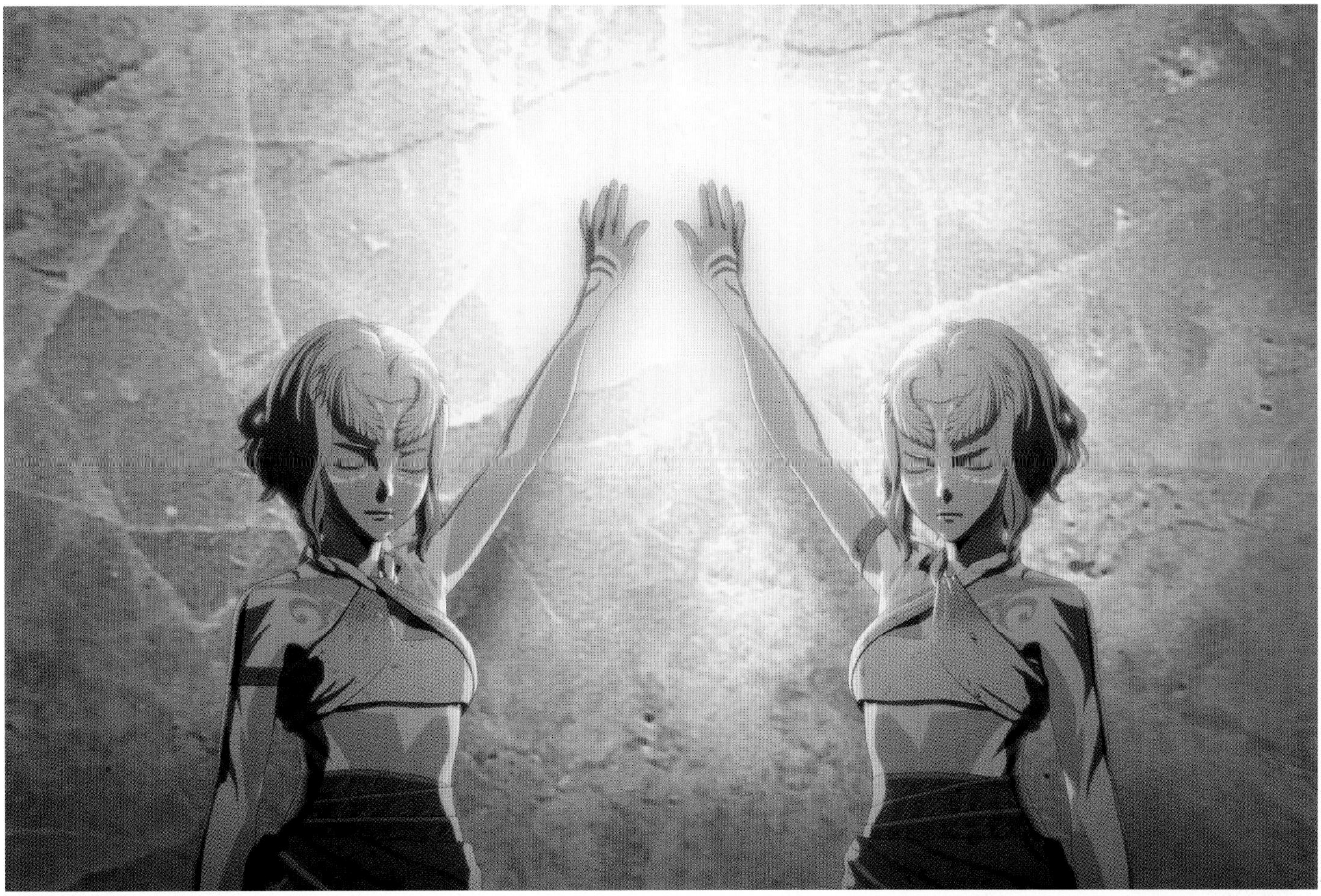

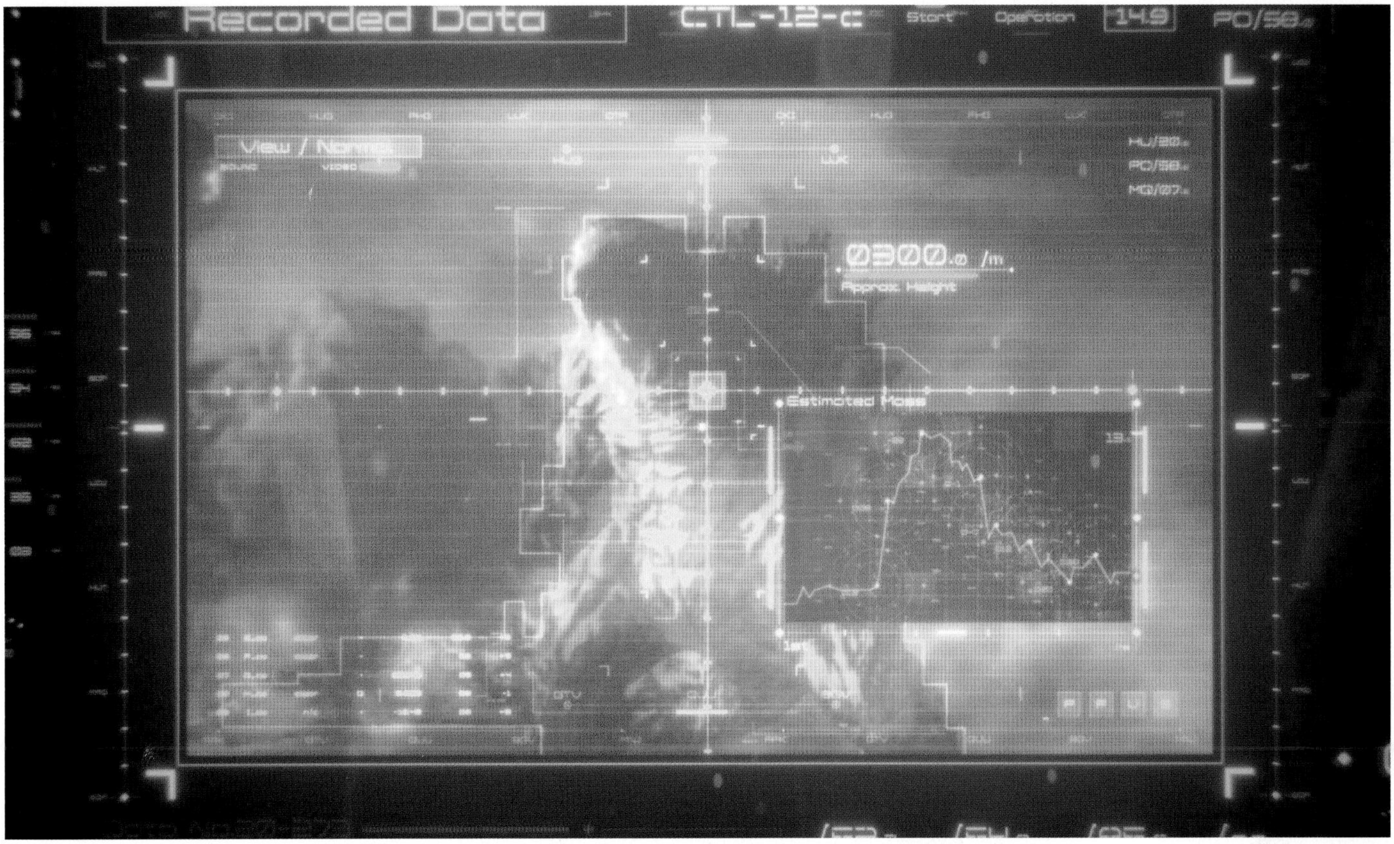
Recorded Data
CTL-12-c
Start
Operation
14.9
View / Normal
Approx. Height
Estimated Mass

GODZILLA 星を喰う者

GODZILLA: THE PLANET EATER (2018)

DIRECTOR : HIROYUKI SESHITA, KOBUN SHIZUNO
WRITTEN BY : GEN UROBUCHI
PRODUCED BY : TAKASHI YOSHIZAWA
SCORE : TAKAYUKI HATTORI
STARRING : MAMORU MIYANO, TAKAHIRO SAKURAI, KANA HANAZAWA, TOMOKAZU SUGITA, YUKI KAJI

THE FINAL INSTALMENT OF GODZILLA'S ANIMATED TRILOGY TAKES THE AUDIENCE FROM A WORLD DOMINATED BY TECHNOLOGY TO ONE FILLED WITH MYSTICISM, PHILOSOPHY, AND QUESTIONING THE VERY NATURE OF GOD.

In the wake of Haruo's destruction of Mechagodzilla City, the Bilusaludo aliens revolt, believing that Earth's only hope of destroying Godzilla had lain in the nanotechnology present. Of course, the uber-religious Exif (as well as the humans) believe that the Bilusaludo were only interested in assimilating Earth through their nanomachines. This rift between factions causes the Bilusaludo aliens to turn on their onetime allies, and shut off the power to the mother ship until the others bow to their demands. One Exif priest – the enigmatic Metphies – however, has other plans.

Metphies, along with his fellow believers, summons their god to Earth to cleanse it of Godzilla. What Haruo and the others soon realize, however, is that their god will not only cleanse the earth of Godzilla, it will cleanse the earth of *everything*. Including all life on it.

It turns out that their god is King Ghidorah, the same beast that ravaged the Exif world so long ago. Why worship a god that promises life after death when you can worship a god that brings death itself? Through prayer and a mysterious stone, Metphies is able to summon King Ghidorah across space, time, and reality itself to Earth for a final battle with Earth's protector, Godzilla.

The Ghidorah we see in this film is unlike any other in Toho's history. It is represented as an extra-dimensional being with three infinitely long heads that exist both within our dimension and not: they are able to bite and siphon energy from Godzilla while not allowing Godzilla to attack them. A seemingly unstoppable foe.

Haruo learns that Metphies is psychically linked with Godzilla and Ghidorah, and has offered up the planet as sacrifice to his god. Both he and Metphies engage in a psychic battle of wills, which Metphies would surely win were it not for the twins interfering, asking their deity (who fans immediately recognize as Mothra) to free Haruo from Metphies' psychic grasp.

With the psychic link broken, Godzilla is free to battle Ghidorah, and the planet is once again safe in the hands of her greatest protector.

Godzilla: The Planet Eater takes many concepts from the Godzilla franchise and uses them to ask big questions. What is the "God" in "Godzilla?" What is the difference between worshiping technology and worshiping a destructive deity? How do we find balance and peace within a world that we helped destroy? How does humanity grapple with its "original sin" of the atomic bomb?

This film asks these questions and provides thoughtful counters to each of them, showcasing this metaphysical query of a movie through ethereal and psychedelic imagery, fully utilizing the singular abilities of animation to tell the story. By the end, we are left with the essential lesson that no matter how advanced we become as a species, and no matter how obsessed or driven we are with mortal concepts such as revenge, honor, or faith, we are ultimately at the mercy of the planet. Earth is our home, and Godzilla is the embodiment of nature itself. Life-giving and deadly, brutal and beautiful.

These themes exemplify Godzilla, and as Toho steps forward into this new era, they have clearly started off on the right foot with bold choices in storytelling without sacrificing the soul of what makes Godzilla so special. This latest film of the Reiwa Era shows that Godzilla is alive and well in the hands of its home studio, and assures us that however we see it again, it will certainly be unexpected.

Just as Haruo's final moments in his Vulture Mecha become immortalized in Earth's mythic history, so too has Godzilla become more than simply a movie monster. It is a living, breathing legend, one that may lay dormant for many years, but that will eventually rise again to destroy, save, and inspire.

Opposite (top): King Ghidorah emerges from another dimension.

Opposite (middle left): Godzilla prepares its heat ray.

Opposite (middle right): Power surges around Godzilla as it builds up energy.

Opposite (bottom left): A seemingly-infinite, extra-dimensional King Ghidorah is able to phase in and out of the physical plane as it battles Godzilla.

Opposite (bottom right): Godzilla and King Ghidorah locked in epic battle.

ゴジラ
メカゴジラ

THE AMERICAN FILMS

Since the original *Godzilla* in 1954, American audiences have been obsessed with the King of the Monsters. Hollywood studios had long collaborated with Toho to bring Godzilla stateside, often re-editing and sometimes re-shooting parts of the films to 'Americanize' the movies before they hit cinemas in the US. It wasn't until 1998 that Hollywood was able to make its own Godzilla film, putting a uniquely American spin on the Japanese movie legend. The four films produced by American studios represent a new chapter for Godzilla, ranging from the totally unexpected and different, to nostalgic reverence, and even resurrecting a classic Toho monster brawl. Enter the mysterious Monarch Sciences, MUTOs, and a divisive – however memorable – tuna-hungry building climber with a home base in Madison Square Garden...

ゴジラ

GODZILLA (1998)

DIRECTOR : ROLAND EMMERICH
WRITTEN BY : ROLAND EMMERICH, DEAN DEVLIN
PRODUCED BY : DEAN DEVLIN
SCORE : DAVID ARNOLD, MICHAEL LLOYD
STARRING : MATTHEW BRODERICK, JEAN RENO, MARIA PITILLO, HANK AZARIA, KEVIN DUNN

ALTHOUGH GODZILLA FILMS HAD BEEN RELEASED IN AMERICA – AND OFTEN HEAVILY EDITED TO DIFFER FROM THEIR JAPANESE ORIGINALS – IT TOOK 44 YEARS FOR AN ORIGINAL GODZILLA FILM TO BE PRODUCED BY A HOLLYWOOD STUDIO.

Producer Henry G. Saperstein, who had distributed a number of Godzilla films in the US in the past, negotiated a deal between Toho Studios and Sony Pictures to produce a trilogy of new Godzilla films in America. Of course, only one film in that planned trilogy actually made it to screens, and it would be helmed by perhaps the pre-eminent name in disaster cinema: Roland Emmerich.

Emmerich's *Godzilla* opens appropriately with a nuclear test in French Polynesia, and an iguana nest becomes irradiated as a result. Shortly thereafter, local fishermen return home traumatized after having encountered some kind of enormous beast. The government wonders if it might be a dinosaur that has survived all these years. Matthew Broderick's Nick Tatopolous, however, believes it to be an iguana mutated by the nuclear fallout.

Eventually, the creature – now dubbed Godzilla after one of the fishermen referred to it as the ancient sea monster Gojira (just like the original film) attacks New York City, wreaking havoc and yet somehow remaining able to elude the military strike forces by hiding in the concrete jungle of skyscrapers, and even tunneling deep underground.

Soon, the film's team of intrepid heroes locates the beast's nest: hundreds of eggs laid in a ruined Madison Square Garden. Dr Tatopolous informs us that Godzilla is able to reproduce asexually, like many reptiles, thereby making Godzilla, for the first time... a mother!

When the military slaughters her brood, Godzilla goes on another rampage through New York City, resulting in a final clash with the military on the Brooklyn Bridge that is both an exciting action set-piece, and tragic end for our favorite monster. Shades of the sad ending of the original *Godzilla* linger, along with a treatment of the monster in a way that reminds us of *King Kong*.

The film had been in development for nearly ten years before finally getting made, much of that time spent with various directors all pitching their own unique ideas for how to reboot *Godzilla* for a modern, western audience. Roland Emmerich and Dean Devlin opted to go in a completely different direction than any of the previous Toho films, taking only the concept of an irradiated monster and then discarding everything else. It would also have a star-studded cast headlined by comedy icon Broderick and The Professional himself, Jean Reno. It would feature an original song from Sean 'Puffy' Combs and Jimmy Page – truly a blockbuster formula to make as big a splash as possible. Emmerich would also dedicate the film to recently-passed Godzilla legend Tomoyuki Tanaka, who was as much responsible for the birth and long life of the world's most famous kaiju as Ishiro Honda. This was a kind gesture, and a thread connecting America's new vision of Godzilla with its Japanese roots.

In this *Godzilla*, the monster would be simply a giant creature – quick, agile, and driven by instinct. Gone would be the mythical majesty of Toho's Godzilla, in favor of a creature merely trying to survive, one that could be outsmarted and ultimately beaten by the minds of scientists and the might of the US military.

Critical and audience response to the film was mostly negative, with audiences failing to respond to the purposefully camp tone of this film, as opposed to the more earnest Toho endeavors. Poor box office returns resulted in the rest of the planned trilogy being scrapped.

In the wake of the disappointing release of the film, Toho would brand this version of Godzilla as simply "Zilla." Why? As longtime Godzilla producer Shogo Tomiyama said: "They took the God out of Godzilla."

It was clear that although Emmerich's film is a fun disaster movie with some of the King of the Monsters' DNA at its heart, fans wanted their mythical kaiju back in the style they'd grown accustomed to over the past 45 years. Toho would quickly reclaim the franchise with the Millennium series, but that didn't mean Hollywood didn't aim to continue lending their voice to the tapestry of Godzilla's mythos.

It would be 16 years before Godzilla would again stomp through Hollywood, this time as part of a newly planned "Monsterverse" from Legendary Pictures...

FROM THE CREATORS OF INDEPENDENCE DAY
GODZILLA
"...an expertly designed theme park ride of a movie that packs non-stop thrills."
SIZE DOES MATTER
Visit www.Godzilla.com
PG-13
COLUMBIA TRISTAR
Printed in U.S.A.

ゴジラ

GODZILLA (2014)

DIRECTOR : GARETH EDWARDS
WRITTEN BY : MAX BORENSTEIN
PRODUCED BY : JON JASHNI, MARY PARENT, BRIAN ROGERS, THOMAS TULL
SCORE : ALEXANDRE DESPLAT
STARRING : AARON TAYLOR-JOHNSON, KEN WATANABE, BRYAN CRANSTON, ELIZABETH OLSEN, SALLY HAWKINS

LEGENDARY PICTURES OBTAINED THE U.S. RIGHTS TO GODZILLA IN 2010, A FULL 12 YEARS SINCE ROLAND EMMERICH LAST BROUGHT HIS VERSION OF THE KING OF THE MONSTERS TO AMERICAN SHORES.

They sought out indie horror auteur Gareth Edwards, whose micro-budget debut feature *Monsters* had wowed audiences the world over through its economical storytelling and focus on the size and scale of the titular monsters threatening the protagonists. The fact that he was able to make the film on a budget of only $500,000 showed them that not only was Edwards adept at telling moving stories of giant creatures, he could do so on a budget.

Thus, Edwards was handed the reigns to reboot *Godzilla* for a modern audience. Edwards reached back to the earliest appearance of Godzilla in Honda's original film, focusing on the dread, weight, and meaning of Godzilla as a character, in addition to allowing it to fight other kaiju, a hallmark of Toho's Godzilla franchise.

The story tells of US Navy Officer Ford Brody, who as a child witnessed disaster when his mother was killed in a nuclear accident at the nearby power plant, which also sent his scientist father on a downward spiral of delusion and paranoia as he tried to uncover the truth behind the tragedy. Years later, as an adult, Brody is reunited with his eccentric father as the truth behind the disaster is revealed: giant monsters are feeding off the nuclear energy.

Apparently, back in 1954 an ancient giant monster resurfaced after millennia asleep, and the subsequent frequent H-bomb tests were not responsible for its mutation, but were instead attempts to kill it. Attempts that were, of course, unsuccessful. But this monster – who we know as Godzilla – was not the only one of these Titans to emerge. Other large creatures, known as MUTOs (Massive Unidentified Terrestrial Organism), have been cocooned and feeding off nuclear power sources for decades, carefully watched and studied by a shadowy scientific research organization known as Monarch.

Eventually, the MUTOs awaken and begin to wreak havoc, prompting a plan by the US military to use nuclear warheads to lure them out to sea for a safe extermination. Of course, everything goes awry, and soon the two MUTOs and Godzilla converge on an unsuspecting San Francisco for a final showdown that proves that Godzilla is – and always has been – the King of the Monsters.

Edwards drenches the film in atmosphere and a true sense of scale, introducing the audience to the largest Godzilla to date, standing at 355 feet tall. Like Ishiro Honda, Edwards makes the audience wait to finally see the monster in all his glory, as he doesn't appear until 55 minutes into the film – over halfway through. Once it arrives, however, the action never lets up and the wait is most definitely worth it.

For only the second time, the King of the Monsters would be a fully CGI creation, using motion capture to craft its performance. Iconic motion capture performer and pioneer Andy Serkis (best known for his work in *The Lord of the Rings* trilogy, the modern *Planet of the Apes* trilogy, and Peter Jackson's *King Kong*) was brought in as a consultant to ensure that not only would Godzilla move with veracity, but that it would have a soul. The result is vastly different from the previous American creation, where instead of a nimble reptile, this Godzilla is a hulking tank of a beast, slow, methodical, and unstoppable. Motion capture performance artist and martial arts master T.J. Storm provided the motion capture performance for Godzilla.

This film was intended to set in motion a new series of interconnected films for Legendary Pictures. Dubbed the Monsterverse, this new series would focus on the kaiju as Titans, ancient beings who used to rule this planet millennia in the past, and who slumber in hidden locations around the world, waiting to be awoken. The secret research organization Monarch would be a common thread throughout these films, which were intended to introduce new monsters in subsequent instalments, not only featuring Godzilla, but Kong as well. Eventually, the hope would be to have the world's two most famous monsters duke it out in spectacular fashion.

The critical and financial success of Edwards' *Godzilla* proved that the world was ready for this new take on the beloved franchise, and immediately the various chess pieces began to be placed that would allow for these monsters to battle it out on the big screen.

Another modern horror icon would be tapped to return us to the world of Godzilla in a sequel film five years later. And this time, Godzilla would be joined by several of its most famous associates.

AARON TAYLOR-JOHNSON
KEN WATANABE
ELIZABETH OLSEN
JULIETTE BINOCHE
SALLY HAWKINS
WITH DAVID STRATHAIRN
AND BRYAN CRANSTON
GODZILLA
WARNER BROS. PICTURES AND LEGENDARY PICTURES PRESENT
A LEGENDARY PICTURES PRODUCTION A GARETH EDWARDS FILM "GODZILLA" AARON TAYLOR-JOHNSON KEN WATANABE ELIZABETH OLSEN JULIETTE BINOCHE SALLY HAWKINS
WITH DAVID STRATHAIRN AND BRYAN CRANSTON MUSIC SUPERVISOR DAVE JORDAN MUSIC BY ALEXANDRE DESPLAT EDITED BY BOB DUCSAY PRODUCTION DESIGNER OWEN PATERSON DIRECTOR OF PHOTOGRAPHY SEAMUS McGARVEY, ASC, BSC
EXECUTIVE PRODUCERS PATRICIA WHITCHER ALEX GARCIA YOSHIMITSU BANNO KENJI OKUHIRA BASED ON THE CHARACTER 'GODZILLA' OWNED AND CREATED BY TOHO CO., LTD. STORY BY DAVID CALLAHAM SCREENPLAY BY MAX BORENSTEIN
PRODUCED BY THOMAS TULL JON JASHNI MARY PARENT BRIAN ROGERS DIRECTED BY GARETH EDWARDS
LEGENDARY
facebook.com/GodzillaMovie
MAY 16
Godzillamovie.com
#Godzilla
SEE IT IN real D 3D AND IMAX 3D

ゴジラ　キング・オブ・モンスターズ

GODZILLA: KING OF THE MONSTERS (2019)

DIRECTOR : MICHAEL DOUGHERTY
WRITTEN BY : MICHAEL DOUGHERTY, ZACH SHIELDS, MAX BORENSTEIN
PRODUCED BY: MARY PARENT, BRIAN ROGERS, THOMAS TULL
SCORE : BEAR MCCREARY
STARRING : KYLE CHANDLER, VERA FARMIGA, MILLIE BOBBY BROWN, KEN WATANABE, ZIYI ZHANG, CHARLES DANCE

THE SAGA OF THE TITANS WAS ONLY JUST BEGINNING, AND POPULAR HORROR DIRECTOR MICHAEL DOUGHERTY – HIMSELF A LIFELONG GODZILLA FAN – WAS BROUGHT ON BOARD TO EXPAND THE LEGENDARY MONSTERVERSE AND LURE GODZILLA INTO BATTLE WITH A FEW OF ITS MOST FAMOUS KAIJU FOES AND FRIENDS.

The film opens in the wreckage of Godzilla's assault on San Francisco from the previous film, following a couple and their young daughter, desperately searching for their missing son in the midst of all the destruction and chaos. Fast-forward five years, and we learn that the son was never found. Now, the father (a former scientist for Monarch) has fled to the wilds to study wolves in blissful isolation, while the mother (Dr. Emma Russell), herself also a scientist with Monarch, raises their daughter (played by *Stranger Things'* Millie Bobby Brown). What's more, Dr. Russell has apparently developed a device capable of communicating with the Titans. With this technology, she can influence these gigantic monsters in unprecedented ways.

However, Godzilla has not been seen in the intervening years. And neither have any of the other Titans. There are factions within Monarch that want to kill the Titans (if they can be found), and others that revere them, trusting them to maintain a global ecological balance.

Dr. Russell is able to test her invention on a larval Mothra, who instantly turns placid when the device is initiated. This gets the attention of an extremist eco-terrorist team led by a villainous Charles Dance that wishes to set the Titans free, awakening all of them to rain destruction on the planet and restore what they believe to be the "natural order". In a stunning twist, it turns out Dr. Russell believes the same thing, and they decide to resurrect the most powerful Titan of all: Monster Zero. This is a beast Godzilla fans know as King Ghidorah.

Amidst all this, Rodan is awakened from a volcanic slumber, and although Godzilla answers the call to battle, King Ghidorah is far too powerful for any of the other Titans to withstand. The unfortunate truth is made clear that King Ghidorah has no interest in maintaining any kind of natural order. King Ghidorah aims to scorch the planet and leave no human or Titan alive.

Dougherty's film focuses as much on the familial tug of war between Millie Bobby Brown's Maddie and Vera Farmiga's Dr. Russell as it does on the battling Titans and even the hierarchy of their kind. Mothra returns as the "Queen of the Monsters," a protector and ally of Godzilla whose appearances seem almost supernatural and ethereal. King Ghidorah is pure evil, snakelike heads slithering and gnashing hungry teeth, aching to destroy for no other reason than murder. Rodan is a wild, dangerous beast, its wings concussive with each flap, and its trail of lava-like fire chaotic and deadly.

And of course, there is Godzilla, hulking, its shoulders weighted with the task of protecting Earth from Titans run amok. More than ever, Godzilla here appears to understand its duty, without relinquishing its inherent power to destroy mankind if it so wishes.

This is indeed a film about monsters and what it takes to be the King.

Bear McCreary's score harkens back to Ifukube's original themes throughout the film, equal parts homage and goosebump-inducing recognition of the mythic power of these characters. Dougherty infuses every second of the film with a deep reverence for the entire franchise, as well as an understanding of why these monsters are more than mere city destroyers. They are gods, and it is only when man forgets humility that they destroy that which we hold dear. When we display a mutual trust and respect, however, we can commune with these creatures, and maybe even learn something from one another.

This film introduces the idea of the Hollow Earth to the Legendary Monsterverse, and ends the closing credits with a foreshadowing cave painting of Godzilla fighting a giant ape-like beast. There is deep history hinted at throughout the film, not simply through cave paintings like this one, but especially in a heartrending moment where we glimpse Godzilla in its home at the bottom of the ocean.

Dougherty infused his take on Godzilla with memory of what came before, while propelling the series ahead on its inevitable trajectory. The next time we would see Godzilla on the big screen would be at the end of an unforeseen global pandemic, with both monsters and audiences clamoring for something big, loud, destructive, and cathartic.

A fight that began in 1962 was about to end once and for all...

GODZILLA
KING OF THE MONSTERS

LONG LIVE THE KING
IN THEATERS **MAY 2019**
LEGENDARY
PG-13
EXPERIENCE IT IN IMAX REAL D 3D DOLBY CINEMA

ゴジラvsコング

GODZILLA VS. KONG (2021)

DIRECTOR : ADAM WINGARD
WRITTEN BY : ERIC PEARSON, MAX BORENSTEIN
PRODUCED BY : THOMAS TULL, ALEX GARCIA, JON JASHNI, ERIC MCLEOD, MARY PARENT, BRIAN ROGERS
SCORE : JUNKIE XL
STARRING : ALEXANDER SKARSGÅRD, MILLIE BOBBY BROWN, REBECCA HALL, BRIAN TYREE HENRY, SHUN OGURI

FOR THE MOST RECENT APPEARANCE OF GODZILLA ON THE BIG SCREEN, ANOTHER INDEPENDENT HORROR DIRECTOR WAS BROUGHT ON BOARD TO BRING TWO ICONIC MONSTERS TOGETHER IN EPIC BATTLE: ADAM WINGARD.

He would use his extensive knowledge of classic action cinema to pit the world's most famous kaiju against one another in a sci-fi/action spectacle that is equal parts Showa Era fun, Heisei Era fantasy, and Millennium Era colorful flashiness. For the first time in almost 60 years, Godzilla and Kong would clash once more.

Set five years after Godzilla's decisive win at the end of *King of the Monsters*, and more than 4 years since we last saw Kong in *Kong: Skull Island*, the world is well aware of the presence of Titans, and Monarch has observation outposts all around the world. They monitor the Titans, many of whom slumber, while others like Godzilla roam their territory, peaceful and quiet ever since Godzilla defeated King Ghidorah.

Kong, having had no part in the events of *Godzilla: King of the Monsters*, has been put into a sort of witness protection program, with Monarch constructing a giant holographic enclosure that they hope will keep Kong happy and blissfully unaware that he is, in effect, in a zoo. Kong is too smart for such a ruse, however, and begins to test the security of his bonds. The reason for such a deception is that if Godzilla were aware of Kong's presence, he would attack as he must maintain his position as the alpha Titan on the planet. And unlike other monsters who would willingly submit to Godzilla, Kong "bows to no one".

Meanwhile, the otherwise peaceful Godzilla suddenly attacks a major tech company's research center, killing hundreds and decimating the compound. It's unfathomable that Godzilla would suddenly turn on mankind, but that indeed appears to be what is happening.

With Kong eager to leave his enclosure, and the threat of a Godzilla attack on the beloved giant ape eminent, the decision is made to use Kong as a guide to find the Hollow Earth – the mythical original home of the Titans that supposedly exists at the center of the planet. When Kong is transported to Antarctica – the first doorway to the Hollow Earth – Godzilla attacks, and it is only the first of many earth-shattering confrontations between the two legendary Titans.

By the end of the film, cities will be leveled, ancient rivalries will be awoken, and even a surprise appearance by a malicious Mechagodzilla will occur! It's nonstop monster action, a testament to Godzilla in its many forms throughout the decades, and a love letter to the big, bold ideas and raucous brawls that made the world fall in love with Godzilla in the first place.

Wingard focused on the characters of Godzilla and Kong first and foremost, wanting us to identify with them as more than just monsters destroying buildings. While Kong is portrayed as a sympathetic being simply trying to survive, Wingard is able to balance having Godzilla as both unstoppable menace and global peacekeeper. It is at once a villain and a hero.

Adam Wingard's experience of making low-budget horror films, with a focus on character, unforgettable visuals, and clever underscoring of humor is evident here. We care about Godzilla and Kong, in different ways befitting their characters. And although Godzilla may not be the sign language-speaking cuddly warrior that Kong is, it displays brains as well as brawn, doing what it must to retain his dominance as well as forging alliances when necessary.

A kaiju-sized box office and streaming success, there is certainly a wondering if Legendary's Monsterverse will continue in its current form. Will we see Godzilla return to fight other iconic monsters? Or will this Godzilla return to the sea, sleeping until the day comes to rise again in a new form? Only time will tell.

The silver screen is not the only home Godzilla has ever known, however. The King of the Monsters has stomped through comics, manga, television, video games, and much more throughout its nearly 70-year history. In the next section, we will explore the great variety of other media that is part of Godzilla's domain.

"FOR THE FIRST TIME IN ALMOST 60 YEARS, GODZILLA AND KONG WOULD CLASH ONCE MORE."

ONE WILL FALL

GODZILLA VS. KONG

SEE IT IN THEATERS | AND ON HBO max

AT NO EXTRA COST TO SUBSCRIBERS

2021

AVAILABLE ON HBO MAX FOR 31 DAYS FROM THEATRICAL RELEASE

金龍山
雷門

GODZILLA IN OTHER MEDIA

While Godzilla will always be best known for its adventures on the silver screen, it has appeared in numerous other formats through the decades. From television, to comic books, and even to video games, the King of the Monsters conquers whatever medium it finds itself in. In this section we'll cover just a few of Godzilla's epic adventures in media other than the movies.

TELEVISION

IN ADDITION TO RAMPAGING THROUGH CINEMAS WORLDWIDE, GODZILLA HAS ALSO GRACED THE SMALL SCREEN, INVADING OUR HOMES IN A VARIETY OF DIFFERENT INCARNATIONS THROUGH THE YEARS. IN THIS SECTION, WE'LL DETAIL MANY OF THE VARIOUS TELEVISION APPEARANCES, AS WELL AS ONE VERY SPECIAL ANIMATED MEETING THAT BECAME FAMOUS THE WORLD OVER...

ZONE FIGHTER (1973)

Godzilla's first foray into television was as a frequent, guest star in Toho's live action *Zone Fighter*, a challenge to the popular *Ultraman* series as well as a televised continuation of the kind of wild monster fighting action fans loved in the Showa Era. In addition to Godzilla, King Ghidorah and Gigan also made appearances in the show, whose continuity is considered canon in the Godzilla universe. The events of the show take place between *Godzilla vs. Megalon* and *Godzilla vs. Mechagodzilla*.

GODZILLA (1978)

Programmed as part of a block of cartoons, classic animation powerhouse Hanna Barbera Studios produced an animated adventure show called simply *Godzilla*. In the show, a team of eco-friendly scientists travels the world on their research boat the *Calico*, encountering dangerous monsters often created by pollution or other man-made disasters. Along for the ride is their friend Godzooky, the silly nephew of Godzilla who may not be able to breathe fire, but can fly due to its tiny wings. When things get too tough for the team to handle, they are able to call on Godzilla to come to the rescue, always prioritizing the safety of people before battling the villainous monsters. Due to television regulations surrounding the property, Godzilla never destroys a building or breathes fire in the direction of people, a stark contrast to the source material but perfect for a half-hour Hanna-Barbera show for children. A generation of kids grew up with the animated *Godzilla*, having seen it as part of its many syndicated hybrid shows like *The Godzilla Power Hour, The Godzilla/Globetrotters Adventure Hour*, or *The Godzilla Super 90*.

GODZILLALAND (1992)

This short-lived educational children's animated series used cute "chibi" style monsters to teach kids everything from singing to aerobic workouts to mathematics. It tied into the upcoming release of the Heisei Era *Godzilla vs. Mothra*. Also called *Adventure! Godzilland*, it proved so popular that a few years later the show was resurrected to help promote *Godzilla vs. Mechagodzilla II*.

GODZILLA ISLAND (1997)

In the late 1990s, a quirky television series called *Godzilla Island* began a run of 256 episodes, each three minutes or less in length. The show functioned as a showcase for new and classic Bandai action figures, as all of the monsters in the show (which comprised most of the cast, as very few humans appeared) were 'played' by action figures manipulated by off-screen hands. The storylines varied in length from only three short episodes to the final arc of over 20, and featured various recognizable kaiju action figures battling each other in a number of locales and with added animation and special effects. No doubt the show inspired many children to buy toys from the Bandai line, a brand that due to the show kept creating fun new original figures that kids could add to their kaiju roster.

GODZILLA: THE SERIES (1998)

In the wake of the box office failure of Roland Emmerich's *Godzilla* in 1998, the two planned sequels were scrapped in favor of a half-hour animated adventure show that would continue the story of the irradiated iguana and the team of scientists and reporters that studied it. In this show, Dr. Nick Tatopolous (the character played by Broderick in the film but recast here) discovers that one of Godzilla's eggs was in fact not destroyed in Madison Square Garden, and to his dismay it has hatched and imprinted on him, thinking he is its father! Protecting the young, new Godzilla (who although a child is still as large as a building), they are able to thwart the destructive plans of other monsters that suddenly arise around the globe. Meanwhile, dastardly government agencies seek to find and destroy the monster, so the team of humans must protect it at all costs. It's a fun action and eco-centric show reminiscent of other '90s era animated adventure shows like *Captain Planet, X-Men,* or *Gargoyles.*

"DR. NICK TATOPOLOUS DISCOVERS THAT ONE OF GODZILLA'S EGGS WAS IN FACT NOT DESTROYED IN MADISON SQUARE GARDEN, AND TO HIS DISMAY IT HAS HATCHED AND IMPRINTED ON HIM, THINKING HE IS ITS FATHER!"

BAMBI MEETS GODZILLA (1969)

A strange jewel in the Godzilla franchise is Marv Newland's animated short film *Bambi Meets Godzilla*, wherein Bambi spends the entirety of a long credits sequence peacefully eating flowers, at the end of which Godzilla's giant foot unceremoniously squashes the beloved fawn. The comedic short not only launched Newland's career as an animator in Hollywood, but would prove so popular that it was included as a special short preceding the US release of *The Return of Godzilla* (aka *Godzilla 1985*).

GODZILLA SINGULAR POINT (2021)

A haunted house. A mysterious signal that could be alien contact. A pteradon from another dimension...

Announced at the end of 2020, *Godzilla Singular Point* is a Netflix original anime series that follows a group of young genius inventors who use their talents to battle otherworldly creatures. As giant monsters begin to appear in the skies, the seas, and the deep caverns of the world, a ragtag team of scientists bands together to figure out the solution to the puzzle of why all of this is happening. One crotchety old inventor, Goro, has built a piecemeal mecha he has named Jet Jaguar (the long-awaited return of the fan favorite robot!), which proves itself on the battlefield versus an angry Rodan and Anguirus. Once sophisticated A.I. is implanted into the robot, it becomes a much more formidable foe - perhaps even one to take on the legendary, world-ending Godzilla.

Meanwhile, scientists studying the strange "red dust" that seems to accompany these massive creatures have discovered the presence of dimensional rifts that may explain the sudden appearance of the deadly monsters around the globe.

This series is energetic and pumped full of admiration and love for the franchise, while taking it in a wholly new and inventive direction. Twists, turns, unique kaiju designs, and its lovable anime characters make this show an – ahem – *singular* addition to the Godzilla canon.

Opposite: Godzilla and Godzooky from Hanna -Barbera's *Godzilla* cartoon.

Top: A battle scene from 1998's underrated *Godzilla: The Series.*

Above: *Godzilla: The Series'* version of Godzilla perched atop the Empire State Building

MANGA AND COMIC BOOKS

GODZILLA HAS A LONG HISTORY ON THE PAGE AS WELL AS THE SCREEN, APPEARING IN DOZENS OF COLLECTIONS OF BOTH AMERICAN COMICS AND JAPANESE MANGA.

The Japanese began adapting Godzilla into black-and-white manga almost from day one, in 1954 to coincide with the release of the original film. For the most part, these manga were adaptations of the films, and often there were several variations of even that! From the original *Godzilla* until *Godzilla 2000: Millennium*, every film (except for *King Kong vs. Godzilla*) received at least one – often more – adaptations in manga form.

The titles vary slightly (for example, *Godzilla vs. Mothra* was renamed *Godzilla vs. Mothra: Great Study* for its manga publishing), and some of the details changed from screen to page, but fans loved the portability and accessibility of their favorite films, especially in the age before home video. For a generation, manga was a Godzilla fan's only way to experience the King of the Monsters without having to wait for a new film or a re-release in a theatre.

Of course, direct adaptations of the films weren't the only adventures Godzilla was having on the manga page – many original tales were spun that continued Godzilla's adventures in an ever-expanding mythos that achieved things the films never could. Godzilla even forayed into other genres, like ultra-violent horror, comedy, and even erotica! The sky was truly the limit for Godzilla fans of all tastes.

In the US, Godzilla has received reverential treatment in the comics industry as well, first appearing in 1976 as part of a limited promotional comic book adaptation of *Godzilla vs. Megalon* – a comic that infamously misnamed Jet Jaguar and Gigan as "Robotman" and "Borodan", respectively.

From there, Dark Horse Comics purchased the rights to adapt Godzilla for American comic readers, and for over a decade published adventures that ranged from English translations of Japanese manga, adaptations of the Godzilla films, and battles with all-new opponents, including an Iron Man-esque Hero Zero, the legendary Spanish Armada, and this author's personal favorite, NBA superstar Charles Barkley!

We're not joking. *Godzilla vs. Charles Barkley* was published in December 1993.

Since 2010, IDW Publishing have been the steward of Godzilla on the comic book page. They have pitted Godzilla against its most famous foes throughout their many issues and releases. All of the favorites are there, from all eras, and Godzilla has fought them on Earth, in space, and even across time. Their decade-long run has been epic in scale, utilized some of the very best talent in the field, and has brought Godzilla to life in bright colors and bold visuals (the images in this section are from IDW's iconic run). Through IDW, Godzilla has also continued to help the people of Japan: in 2011 they released a one-shot collection of 100 variant covers for *Godzilla: Kingdom of Monsters*, with proceeds going to benefit tsunami relief after the Fukushima tragedy.

Seeing Godzilla on the big and small screens is certainly a thrilling experience, but the tactile and portable nature of comics gives fans an entirely new way to behold their beloved monsters. Yet more avenues await, however, for fans that want to get even more hands on. With new technology, it became possible to control the kaiju themselves with the press of a button...

Left: *Godzilla: History's Greatest Monster*. Art by Simon Gane. Colors by Ronda Pattison.

Opposite: *Godzilla: Rage Across Time #5*. Artwork by Bob Eggleton.

Above: From *Godzilla: Cataclysm*. Artwork by Dave Wachter.

Left: *Godzilla: History's Greatest Monster*. Artwork by Simon Gane. Colors by Ronda Pattison.

Opposite (above): *Godzilla: The Half-Century War*. Artwork by James Stokoe.

Opposite (below left): *Godzilla: Rulers of Earth*. Artwork by Matt Frank.

Opposite (below right): *Godzilla: History's Greatest Monster*. Artwork by Dave Wachter.

!!
GUH!
!!!

IDW
GODZILLA
MOWRY
FRANK
PATTISON

Above: *Godzilla: History's Greatest Monster*. Artwork by Zach Howard. Colors by Nelson Daniel.

Right: *Godzilla: Rulers of Earth*. Artwork by Jeff Zornow.

Above (right): *Godzilla: Cataclysm.* Art by Bob Eggleton

Above (left): *Godzilla: Rage Across Time.* Artwork by Tadd Galusha

Left: *Godzilla: History's Greatest Monster.* Artwork by Arthur Adams. Colors by Peter Doherty.

Opposite (above right): *Godzilla: Gangsters & Goliaths.* Artwork by Geof Darrow. Colors by Peter Doherty.

Opposite (above left): *Godzilla Legends.* Artwork by E.J. Su. Colors by Priscilla Tramontano.

Opposite (bottom left): *Godzilla: Rulers of Earth.* Artwork by Jeff Zornow.

Opposite (bottom right): *Godzilla: Cataclysm.* Artwork by Dave Wachter.

IDW
#1 • $3.99 • CVR A
LAYMAN
PONTICELLI
FOTOS
GODZILLA
GANGSTERS & GOLIATHS

IDW
MOWRY
FRANK
TRAMONTANO
GODZILLA

VIDEO GAMES

BEGINNING IN 1983, GODZILLA STOMPED ITS WAY ONTO THE SMALL SCREEN IN A MILITARY STRATEGY GAME FOR THE COMMODORE 64 VIDEO GAME SYSTEM. SINCE THEN, IT'S GONE ON TO STAR, OR APPEAR AS A SURPRISE GUEST IN, DOZENS OF POPULAR VIDEO GAMES WORLDWIDE, FOR SYSTEMS AS WIDE-RANGING AS THE NINTENDO, SUPER NINTENDO, SEGA SATURN, PLAYSTATION, AND EVEN ON OUR PHONES.

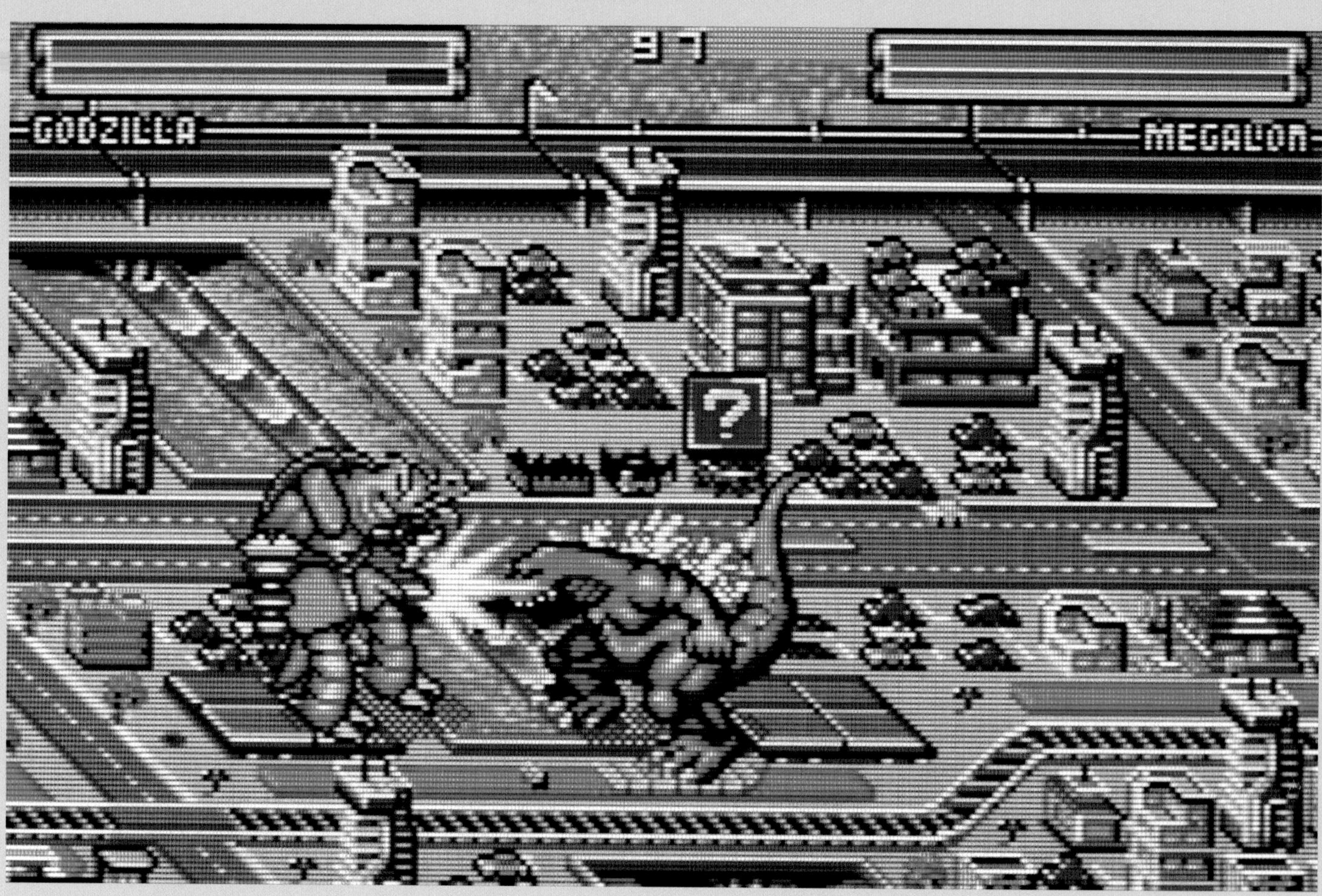

It's also been a popular character in Japan's pachinko gambling machines, as well as pinball and arcade cabinets in video arcades around the world.

There's a unique pleasure to being able to control the military and strategizing ways to destroy Godzilla before it reaches Tokyo (as is the case with the original Commodore 64 *Godzilla*). Equally as fun are titles like 2014's *Godzilla*, where you get to control Godzilla itself as you ravage cities and fight other famous kaiju from the Godzilla universe.

In addition to the plethora of video games where Godzilla has found a home, fans can find it in card games and board games, and even a version of the tower-destroying game *Jenga*! Its evolution from terrifying analogy for the atomic bomb to family-friendly, kaiju-fighting anti-hero is felt more strongly than ever in its life as a star of games, both of the video variety and as one that families gather around the table to play. We all have a kaiju inside us that wants to smash some buildings once in a while, and the decades of Godzilla games have allowed us the freedom to do just that, from the comfort of our own homes...

1.

2.

3.

4.

5.

6.

Opposite: *Godzilla Domination*, Nintendo Game Boy Advance Videogame.

1: *Godzilla: Destroy All Monsters Melee*, Nintendo Gamecube and Xbox.

2: *Super Godzilla* for the Super Nintendo Entertainment System start screen.

3: Godzilla: Monster War for the Super Famicom.

4: The Nintendo Entertainment System's *Godzilla: Monster of Monsters!* Start screen.

5: 1994's *Godzilla: Monster War* for the Super Famicom.

6: The SNES's unusual strategy take on *Super Godzilla*'s gameplay.

CLOSING

For nearly seven decades, Godzilla has destroyed cities, traveled to space, fought giant robots, gone back in time, and even raised a child. It has avenged tragic deaths, sacrificed itself for the greater good, and protected Earth from the likes of evil aliens, angry cultists, and polluting mega corporations. In doing so, it became one of cinema's most recognizable icons, a fascinating creature both feared and beloved, and adored by children and adults.

There is so much depth and complexity layered in the Godzilla franchise, all in a big rubber suit made of pure fun family entertainment. It is truly unique in its ability to instill powerful social messages while also existing as exciting popcorn-fuel adventure, and that's why the Godzilla franchise has endured for so long, and will continue to do so for as long as there are screens for the monster to stomp across.

We tip our hats to the King of the Monsters, the hero that began a villain, and that has worked its way into all of our hearts. It wades off now into the sea, sun burning low on the horizon, but perhaps it'll be back. One day when we need it most – whether as protector against some mythic threat, or to remind us that nature needs to be respected – it'll rise again from the churning waters of Tokyo Bay, that familiar deafening roar rattling our windows and letting us know that Godzilla is on its way...

INDEX

ACKNOWLEDGMENTS/CREDITS

The publishers would like to thank the following sources for their kind permission to reproduce the pictures in this book.

Alamy Stock Photo: AA Film Archive: 233; Album: 31 (poster); ArcadeImages: 250, 251TL, 251TR, 251L, 251R, 251BL, 251BR; BFA: 235, 237; Columbia TriStar Television/Everett Collection Inc: 241T, 241B; Moviestore Collection Ltd: 240; TriStar Pictures/Everett Collection, Inc.: 231

Every effort has been made to acknowledge correctly and contact the source and/ or copyright holder of each picture. Any unintentional errors or omissions will be corrected in future editions of this book.

Following page: One of the original publicity stills for the 1954 film.

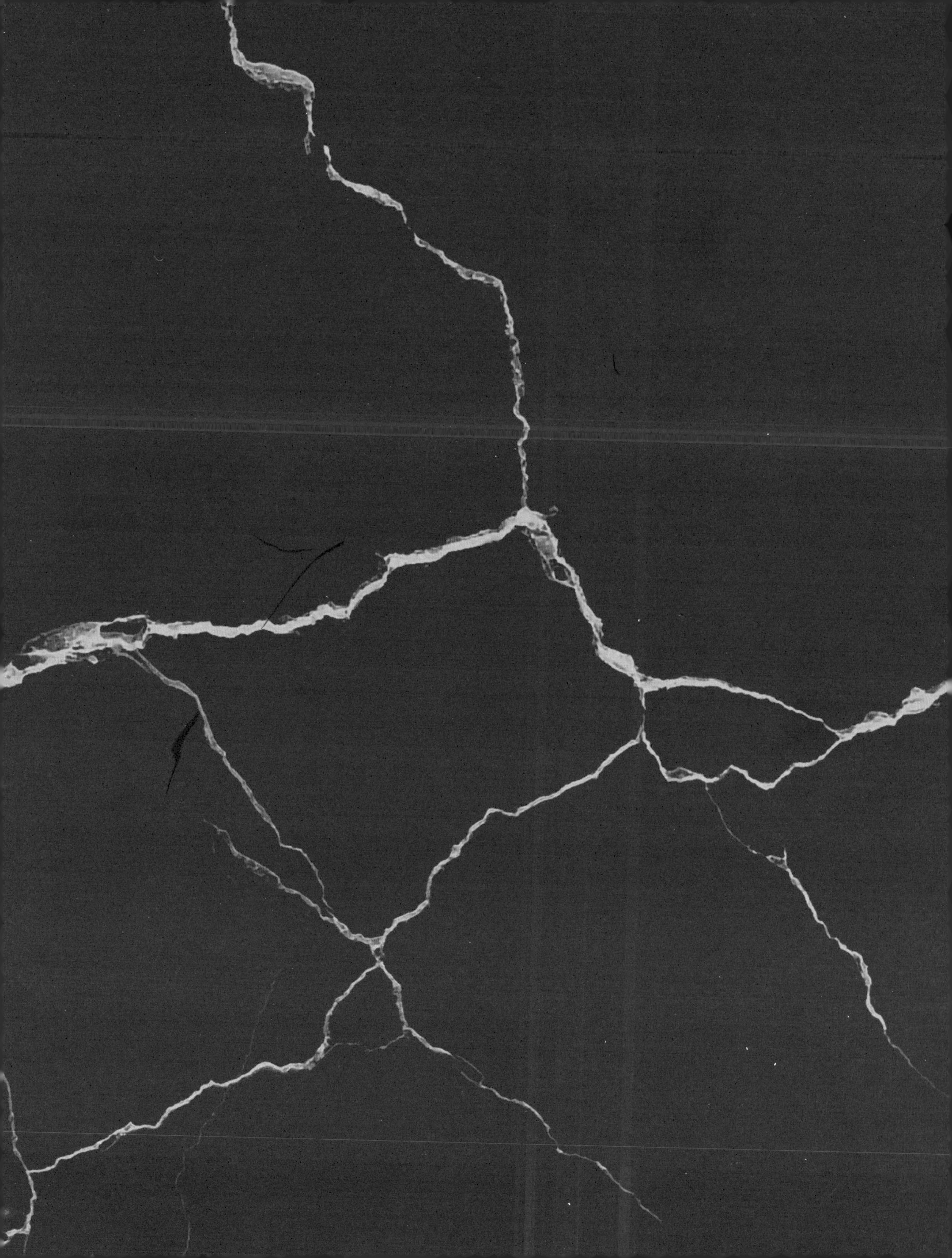